In the Beginning
Was the End

And after the end there is a new Beginning

In the Beginning
Was the End

And after the end there is a new Beginning

Wim Malgo

Table of Contents

Chapter III

Chapter IV

We are glad you have chosen to read this book. It is the deep desire of our hearts that through the message contained in this book you will receive a decisive blessing. Jesus Christ, the Son of God, stated, "I am the door: by me if any man enter in, he shall be saved" (John 10:9). This statement is a wonderful promise and assurance. The word "door," however, also indicates that it serves a certain purpose: it can be closed. We believe this will happen very soon because the Second Coming of Jesus is imminent. When that occurs, the time of grace will have come to an end. While writing this, the door of grace is still open, and this book is part of our task to pass on the message of the Bible. Please read this book without any preconceived ideas which would only hinder the simple message of God from entering your heart. The message contained herein is based on the Word of God. We have carefully compared the events happening in our time with the prophecy of the Word of God. The Bible predicted, thousands of years ago, how the world will end. When we compare the statements made today by leading scientists in the fields of politics, religion, economy and the military with the prediction of the Bible, we see with amazement that the end is, indeed, at hand! Should you have any question after reading this book, I invite you to write to me, and I will do my best to answer your question, especially regarding salvation and your spiritual life.

Sincerely yours,

Wim Malgo

Chapter One

The End of the World According to the Bible

We are beginning this book by talking about the end, that is, the end of the world. Actually, this is not a new subject for this thought has been with man since his existence. The world had a beginning, and, naturally, it will have an end. "Why, how and when?" are the questions we need to ask because today, for the first time in history, the world has reached the point whereby it can destroy itself through man's own inventiveness. Further, and this is more important, the Bible, which we consider the Word of God, clearly predicts in unmistakable terms the end of the world. This Bible in its original text is the infallible, inspired, living Word of God. Nowhere else in all of the literature of the world nor in any science available can we find clearer and more direct information about the end of the world than in the Bible.

To anyone who knows the Bible, it is no surprise that the world is about to fall apart literally. Some 3,000 years ago, the Psalmist wrote about it in Psalm 102:26 and 27, *"They shall perish, but thou shalt endure: yea, all of them shall wax old like a garment; as a vesture shalt thou change them, and they shall be changed: But thou art the same, and thy years shall have no end."*

Later we hear it in Hebrews 1:10,11, *"And, Thou, Lord, in the beginning hast laid the foundation of the earth; and the heavens are the works of thine hands: They shall perish; but thou remainest; and they all shall wax old as doth a garment."* These are plain words. The world was created by the words of the Lord, and these words also tell us that it shall perish! This irreversible process of the decay of the planet earth has raised great concern among the leading scientists of our time. Indeed, the world is beginning to worry about its end. A great number of scientists in all countries of the world are working feverishly to identify the cause and possibly find a remedy to avoid the collapse of this world. But because this type of concern is nothing new and it has been prophesied in the Word of God, we will ask the Word of God to give us light into this subject.

The Book of Books

Because we are requested in the Bible, *"Ask me of things to come"* (Isaiah 45:11), we do right to ask the Bible about the end of the world. There is no doubt that the Bible is the climax of all literature that was ever written. It is indeed the Book of *books*! Regarding publication, distribution, age, and spiritual power, there is no piece of literature on the face of the earth to be found equal to the Bible. The Bible stands above, even extremely far above, all others. The spiritual power of the Bible unites itself with those who believe;

that is the source of victorious power for the individual
believer. That is just another proof and testimony of
the divine inspiration of the Bible. Ask Christ! He is
the Word in person; He was nailed to the cross, and He
was ridiculed, mocked and declared dead. But He
lives, and the Bible lives! Just as He, the Living Word
of God arose, the Bible has risen over and again. It is
indestructible. The Bible identifies itself with the
messengers of Jesus Christ and vice versa. Paul
testifies about it in II Corinthians 5:8,9, *"We are confi-
dent, I say, and willing rather to be absent from the
body, and to be present with the Lord. Wherefore we
labor, that, whether present or absent, we may be
accepted of him."* Thus, we can say the Bible is like the
sun—very old and yet very new each day. After each
night, the sun appears again. It overcomes darkness.
It gives light and life and outshines everything else.
The Bible is king in the kingdom of knowledge. It has,
and is itself, the central source of every remaining and
eternal truth. There is no other place on the face of the
earth where we can receive better or more reliable
information of things to come. Indeed, it is an old book.
Some parts are more than 3,300 years old, and yet it is
totally new for him who reads it. We may read it over
and again and gain more and more. The Holy Scripture not only predicts things to come, but it also
presents each individual reader with the unique plan
of salvation. Only this Book is actually able to
transform anyone into eternity, that is, through it one
can find eternal life.

The Prophetic View can be compared with viewing mountains: One does not see the deep valleys in between.

How to Understand Biblical Prophecy

First, let us see the mystery of Biblical prophecy. Biblical prophecy is not written in newspaper style or in book form, which we can follow stage by stage, chapter by chapter, but it is found like a pattern throughout the Holy Scriptures, the Bible. The mystery of it often consists of statements made which are predicting things to come but sometimes span several thousands of years. Oftentimes we read a prophecy which is uttered in one sentence with half of it fulfilled at a given time but the other half fulfilled 2,000 or more years later. Here is an example:

The prophet Isaiah prophesies in chapter 61:1 of the coming of the Lord and of the work He will do. In verse 2 he continues and says in one sentence, *"To proclaim the acceptable year of the Lord, and the day of vengeance of our God."*

Later, the Lord Jesus quoted this prophecy, but He ended with the words, *"To preach the acceptable year of the Lord"* (Luke 4:19). In verse 21 He continued, *"This day is this scripture fulfilled in your ears."* The Lord did not say anything about *"the day of vengeance of our God"* because that was yet to come. Now, almost 2000 years later, we are approaching the day of the wrath of God. Thus we see from the fulfillment of the first part of Isaiah's prophecy to the fulfillment of the last part of it we have at least 2,000 years in between although he utters this prophecy in one sentence.

The Two and Threefold Fulfillment of Biblical Prophecy

The prophets we read about in our Bible were the mouthpiece of God. We can read that in the first verse in the book of Hebrews. There we find the statement that God spoke to the fathers through the prophets. But because God is eternal, the prophets were proclaiming eternal truths. That simply means that we cannot take the prophecies of the prophet and place them into a limited and certain period of time. Therefore, it is of utmost importance to read all of the Bible and to take notice as to whatever the prophets have to say about the end of the world. The words of the prophets, which are the Words of God, often describe events which are uttered in one sentence but are aimed at a time period of thousands of years, as we have seen in the example of Isaiah 61:2. Many times the prophets describe two diverse events under one name or describe it with one picture which allows us to better view the characteristics of that event. Sometimes, almost unnoticeably, they pass over from one theme of prophecy into another. At times they repeat or expand on previous prophetic statements made by others. Occasionally they go into more details or point to a higher fulfillment of the event.

The Lord Jesus Himself, for instance, prophesied

about our days but in the same breath also included the very last and final judgment which is coming upon the world. He could see it from eternal perspectives and was not bound to time and space in His utterance. As far as the Lord was concerned, the judgment over Jerusalem and Israel, which was fulfilled forty years *after* He made the statement, is included in the great judgment of the end time in which we are now living (compare Matthew 24).

The Extended Fulfillment

Very fittingly, we can compare a prophetic view with a view of the mountains. When you stand on top of a mountain, you seem to see the next mountain behind almost touching the one in front. You are able to see mostly the tops of the mountains. But this situation is totally changed when you view these mountains from an airplane. Then you recognize the great valleys in which you see towns, cities, lakes, rivers, fields, etc.

Let us see another example we find in II Samuel 7:12,13 and 16, *"And when thy days be fulfilled, and thou shalt sleep with thy fathers, I will set up thy seed after thee, which shall proceed out of thy bowels, and I will establish his kingdom. He shall build an house for my name, and I will stablish the throne of his kingdom for ever...And thine house and thy kingdom shall be established for ever before thee: thy throne shall be established for ever."* This promise of God to David concerns itself seemingly only with Solomon, the son of David. But reading this promise carefully, we clearly see that this prophecy is pointing much further past the first son, Solomon, to the last son of David, Jesus Christ, who was able to fulfill and will yet fulfill this promise to the fullest extent in the establishment of the 1,000 years kingdom of peace. This final fulfillment is accomplished through the King of Peace, Jesus Christ. But in between these "valleys" we see thousands upon thousands of years.

Another such prophecy made by Isaiah through which the Lord speaks is about the faithful servant Eliakim. *"And it shall come to pass in that day, that I will call my servant Eliakim the son of Hilkiah: And I will clothe him with thy robe, and strengthen him with thy girdle, and I will commit thy government into his hand: and he shall be a father to the inhabitants of Jerusalem, and to the house of Judah. And the key of the house of David will I lay upon his shoulder; so he shall open, and none shall shut; and he shall shut, and none shall open"* (Isaiah 22:20-22). This prophecy clearly pointed to Eliakim, but the extension of that prophecy is pointing to our exalted Lord as we find Him in Revelation 3:7. Here we see the final fulfillment. The Lord Jesus commands, *"And to the angel of the church in Philadelphia write; These things saith he that is holy, he that is true, he that hath the key of David, he that openeth, and no man shutteth; and shutteth, and no man openeth."*

Let us see a further example in Psalm 8:5-9 where David describes the glory which God has given man, *"For thou hast made him a little lower than the angels, and hast crowned him with glory and honour. Thou madest him to have dominion over the works of thy hands; thou has put all things under his feet: All sheep and oxen, yea, and the beasts of the field; The fowl of the air, and the fish of the sea, and whatsoever passeth through the paths of the seas. O Lord our Lord, how excellent is thy name in all the earth!"* But in the book of Hebrews, we see that this is extended to the spiritual man, and it identifies Jesus Christ to be the fulfillment of it. *"But one in a certain place testified, saying, What is man, that thou art mindful of him? or the son of man, that thou visitest him? Thou madest him a little lower than the angels; thou crownedst him with glory and honour, and didst set him over the works of thy hands: Thou hast put all things in subjection under his feet. For in that he put all in subjection under him, he left nothing that is not put under him. But now we see not yet all things put under him. But we see Jesus, who was made a little lower than the angels for the suffering of death, crowned with glory and honour; that he by the grace of God should taste death for every man"* (Hebrews 2:6-9). The Apostle Paul uses that same succession and application in I Corinthians 15:27, *"For he hath put all things under his feet. But when he saith all things are put under him, it is manifest that he is excepted, which did put all things under him."*

The Extended
Negative Fulfillment

These are just a few examples of that which we find throughout the entire prophetic Word, the Bible. This type of expanded fulfillment and description can also be found in the negative sense, such as in the description of the king of Tyrus in Ezekiel 28. Here the prophet speaks very clearly about the king of Tyrus, but then he continues and identifies, through the king of Tyrus, Satan himself, who at one time was perfect. *"Thou wast perfect in thy ways from the day that thou wast created, till iniquity was found in thee. By the multitude of thy merchandise they have filled the midst of thee with violence, and thou hast sinned: therefore I will cast thee as profane out of the mountain of God: and I will destroy thee, O covering cherub, from the midst of the stones of fire"* (Ezekiel 28:15,16). If this description applied only to the man, the king of Tyrus, we could rightly say that this is an exaggeration; it is a fantasy. Thus, we must understand it in the same way concerning men of God. About those who loved the Lord, promises were given which extended to the Saviour. Hence it was with men who did evil in the sight of the Lord; over them prophecies were uttered which reached to the father of all evil, Satan himself. The same succession can be seen in Isaiah 14 where the prophet prophesies against the king of Babel. This prophecy, too, continues and reaches to Satan himself therewith describing to us the origin of Satan, *"How*

The Shrine of the Book in the Jerusalem museum where the antique Isaiah scrolls, found in the Dead Sea area, are kept.

art thou fallen from heaven, O Lucifer, son of the morning!" (Isaiah 14:12).

Daniel's description (chapter 8) of the evil enemy and destroyer of God's covenant people continues and extends itself into a prophetic view showing the characteristics of the end-time empire. He shows to us the empire of the Antichrist and his power of destruction in the end-time. While studying the book of the prophet Daniel, one should also carefully read historic books which describe the time between the Old and the New Testaments, otherwise, this prophecy remains clouded.

At one time Daniel prophesied of Antiochus Epiphanes who went so far in his acts of abomination as to sacrifice a swine in the Temple of Jerusalem, there where the sanctuary of God was! Thus Daniel's prophecy has already been fulfilled once, but extended, it will be fulfilled again through the horrible beast which will come to rule the world, that is, the Antichrist.

Timeless End-Time

Prophecies we find in the Old Covenant often can be seen as shadows, or symbolic pictures, which find their actual fulfillment in the New Covenant. Both the Old and the New Covenants form a perfect unity in this matter. The prophecies uttered in the Old Testament do not depend, however, on the New Covenant for their fulfillment. Thus we see in Biblical prophecy that often a description seemingly ignores the millennia in between and immediately speaks about the new earth thereby disregarding thousands of years.

Summarizing, we come to the following conclusion: According to the teaching and the statements of the Lord Jesus Christ and His Apostles, the end-time is comprised of His first coming, His second coming and the end of the end-time. Thus the Word of God was fulfilled in time past, it is fulfilling itself today, and it will be fulfilled in the future! The succession of the end-time, therefore, can be described in three categories:

1. The end of the time of the world;
2. The end of its substance;
3. The end of its existence.

The World at the End of Its Time

"I am with you alway, even unto the end of the world" (Matthew 28:20) are words which tell us that there is an end to come. In Ephesians 1:21 we read, *"Not only in this world, but also in that which is to come."* Thus, we see there is a time when the world will end, and all things will be done away with. The time which we call "history" had its beginning at some time, but that time ran out and it is now past. History has seen great things; tremendous events took place, but that is also valid for the future. The very first sentence of our

Bible says, *"In the beginning God created the heaven and the earth"* (Genesis 1:1). We do not know about this creation and there is no further report about it in the Bible, but the next sentence reads, *"And the earth was without form, and void"* (Genesis 1:2). To translate this sentence more precisely it should say, "The earth *became* without form and void." After the first creation, the fall of Satan occurred. The earth participated in this fall to such an extent that it became *"without form, and void."* After this period of time we read in Genesis 1:1 and 2 that God, with the Holy Spirit through His Word, began to recreate the earth in six working days. He created heaven and earth, and prepared it for man. The history of man following that early beginning can be categorized in three parts:

1. From the creation of man until the Flood;
2. From the Flood to the coming of Jesus Christ;
3. From the returning of Christ, the subsequent judgment, the coming millennium to the appearing of the new heaven and the new earth.

The Bible reports that the first dispensation ended with a catastrophic judgment using the element of water. In the same way the Bible predicts about the present time which will also end in catastrophic judgment, but this time through the element of fire. After that something new will be created.

These new beginnings, these radically new conditions, are casting their shadows ahead and are marked by the successive breakdown of the old structure of society today. Alexander Solzhenitsyn, who was expelled from the U.S.S.R., once said very fittingly:

> We are standing at the edge of a historic collapse which is threatening our entire civilization with absolute destruction. Modern society is hypnotized by delusion and self-deception and has lost the sense for danger. Our society is in bondage to materialism. Nothing seems more important than consumer goods and entertainment. In this condition, society is unable to recognize the danger which is approaching.

Whenever something new is to come, the old will have to be done away with. Over this present world, we can quote with assurance the words, "Mene, Mene, Tekel," which means, *"Thou art weighed in the balances, and art found wanting"* (Daniel 5:27). That is the time we are living in, a time of transition. While everything still seems to be working smoothly and we are seemingly finding answers to our problems, something totally new is in the making. The time of prosperity we have known in the past will not return, and if it does, it will only be temporary. One thing is for certain: the world is approaching a dark and terrible time. Whoever reads his Bible carefully knows what is to come. The Bible speaks a very clear language in this matter. But we must point out that as believers, as those who are born-again of the Spirit of God, we are not looking for signs. We already see, optically, the one and only sign of the time: Israel!

ETHIOPIAN

እስመ ፡ ከመዝ ፡ አፍቀር ፡ እግዚአብሔር ፡
ለዓለም ፡ እስከ ፡ ወልደ ፡ ዋሕደ ፡ ወሀበ ፡ ቢዘ ፡
ከመ ፡ ኩሉ ፡ ዘየአምን ፡ ቦቱ ፡ ኢይትሐጐል ፡
አላ ፡ ይረክብ ፡ ሕይወተ ፡ ዘለዓለም ፡፡

ARABIC

لِأَنَّهُ هٰكَذَا أَحَبَّ ٱللّٰهُ ٱلْعَالَمَ حَتَّى بَذَلَ ٱبْنَهُ ٱلْوَحِيدَ لِكَيْ
لَا يَهْلِكَ كُلُّ مَنْ يُؤْمِنُ بِهِ بَلْ تَكُونُ لَهُ ٱلْحَيٰوةُ ٱلْأَبَدِيَّةُ ◆

GERMAN

Also hat Gott die Welt geliebt, daß Er Seinen ein-
geborenen Sohn gab, auf daß alle, die an lhn glauben,
nicht verloren werden, sondern das ewige Leben
haben.

ESPERANTO

Car Dio tiel amis la mondon, ke li donis sian sole-
naskitan Filon, por ke ciu, kiu kredas je li, ne pereu,
sed havu eternan vivon.

FRENCH

Car Dieu a tellement aimé le monde, qu'il a donné
son Fils unique, afin que quiconque croit en lui ne
périsse point, mais qu'il ait la vie éternelle.

The most translated book in the world.
The entire Bible and parts of the Bible are translated in over
1,600 languages. *"For God so loved the world, that he gave his
only begotten Son, that whosoever believeth in him should not*

HEBREW

כִּי־אַהֲבָה רַבָּה אָהַב הָאֱלֹהִים אֶת־הָעוֹלָם עַד־
אֲשֶׁר נָתַן אֶת־בְּנוֹ אֶת־יְחִידוֹ לְמַעַן אֲשֶׁר לֹא־יֹאכַד
כָּל־הַמַּאֲמִין בּוֹ כִּי אִם־יִחְיֶה חַיֵּי עוֹלָם:

RUSSIAN   Russland

Ибо так возлюбил Бог мир, что отдал Сына Своего
единородного, дабы всякий, верующий в Него, не
погиб, но имел жизнь вечную.

TOBA DIALECT

FLEMISH

Want alzoo heeft God de wereld bemind, dat Hij zijn
eeniggeboren Zoon heeft gegeven, opdat al wie in
Hem gelooft niet verga, maar het eeuwige leven heb-
be.

CHINESE

perish but have everlasting life" (John 3:16). Translations of this
verse are shown here in the following languages: Ethiopian,
Arabic, German, Esperanto, French, Hebrew, Russian, Toba
dialect, Flemish, and Chinese.

Israel, The Sign

The Bible teaches that when the Jews return from all the nations back to the Promised Land there will be a sign accompanying their return, namely, the desert shall blossom. But this sign is also synchronized with the return of Jesus Christ. Thus, the end of the Church of Jesus is standing at the door. Our time, the time of the Church, lies exactly between the dispersion of Israel and their return. God indeed rejected Israel, and the Jews were dispersed into all the world. That was the beginning of the time of the Church of Jesus Christ. But that time has begun to end with the return of Israel. *"God at the first did visit the Gentiles, to take out of them a people for his name"* (Acts 15:14); but then we read, *"After this I will return, and will build again the tabernacle of David, which is fallen down"* (verse 16). That is the reacceptance of Israel by God which is being visibly illustrated for us through Israel, and, therewith, we know that the time of grace is coming to an end for the Church of Jesus. We point out, the Church of Jesus Christ is not limited to any denomination but consists of all individual believers who are born-again. When we speak about the Church we do not mean the organization but the organism.

The war in Iran, the immense suffering in Cambodia, the endless genocide in Uganda or the recent problems in Poland are not the most important items on the agenda for the United Nations. This organization, which consists of almost all the nations of the world, was brought about as an attempt to solve the problems of the world. But they do little, if anything, when thousands, even hundreds of thousands of innocent people are murdered. Yet if anything happens in Israel, especially in Jerusalem, no matter how small, it immediately becomes subject number one for the U.N. Why is this so? Answer: because God Himself has made Jerusalem to be *"a cup of trembling"* and *"a burdensome stone"* for all people according to Zechariah 12:2,3. The United Nations and, strangely enough, the World Council of Churches, reject the absolute authority of the Bible, and, therefore, they do not know what to do with Jerusalem. That is why Jerusalem is a cup of trembling and a burdensome stone for them. Because the indisputable authority of the Bible is rejected, the people who are in charge of the World Security Council have, in actual fact, become a World Insecurity Council. Thus they are being molded to accept anyone who can produce security, and, therewith, they are preparing for the rule of the Antichrist. We know that this short rule of horror by the Antichrist will end in judgment, and through it the kingdom of Jesus Christ, the Messiah of God, will be established. Because the rule of the Antichrist and the kingdom of God are approaching, the end-time in which we now live is in a state of utter confusion. Anyone not accepting the authority of the Bible is puzzled as to why things are going the way they are. The world does not know that it is beginning to taste the cup of trembling, Jerusalem, because they are burdening themselves with the burdensome stone, Jerusalem.

The Moral Degeneration and Apostasy

Apostasy from the living faith in God is a typical symptom of our time. As a result, one is unable to permit the Holy Spirit of God to correct one. Humanity is serving the creation rather than the Creator. Man is stubbornly refusing to believe in the invisible power of the eternal God. That is also the fundamental reason why homosexuality is spreading like cancer in our society. Certain medical scientists are dead wrong when they assume that homosexuality is a sickness for which a cure must be found. The reason for homosexuality can be found in the Bible; it is rejection of God. *"Because that, when they knew God, they glorified him not as God, neither were thankful; but became vain in their imaginations, and their foolish heart was darkened. Professing themselves to be wise, they became fools, And changed the glory of the uncorruptible God into an image made like to corruptible man, and to birds, and fourfooted beasts, and creeping things. Wherefore God also gave them up to uncleanness through the lusts of their own hearts, to dishonor their own bodies between themselves: Who changed the truth of God into a lie, and worshipped and served the creature more than the Creator, who is blessed forever.*

Amen. For this cause God gave them up unto vile affections: for even their women did change the natural use into that which is against nature: And likewise also the men, leaving the natural use of the woman, burned in their lust one toward another; men with men working that which is unseemly, and receiving in themselves that recompence of their error which was meet" (Romans 1:21-27).

This old book, the Bible, is indeed up-to-date! If our medical science would search for the true reason, then they would already know the cure: back to the Bible! Others in our highly educated society are describing homosexuality and other perverse acts as normal, as a matter of choice and preference. This direction of thinking obviously results in pressure on the normal, healthy family life: if homosexuality is not wrong, then something may be wrong with our traditional family value! Why has our society gone this far? Because they have not kept the Bible as the supreme and proper authority for man's actions, thoughts, and deeds. Very fittingly Proverbs 13:13 says, *"Whoso despiseth the word shall be destroyed."* Luther translates this, "Whoso despises the word destroys himself." In many countries (among them is Holland), it is permitted by law and considered normal for two men to marry, and that in a church! We ask, "How long can God tolerate such abominable deeds of man?" It will not be long, for destruction will come suddenly as the Lord Jesus has prophesied, *"Likewise also as it was in the days of Lot* [homosexuality was apparently legalized]; *they did eat, they drank, they bought, they sold, they planted, they builded; But the same day that Lot went out of Sodom it rained fire and brimstone from heaven, and destroyed them all. Even thus shall it be in the day when the Son of man is revealed"* (Luke 17:28-30). Immorality has reached proportions never known heretofore.

Unrighteousness is another item which is taking on frightening proportions. That, too, was prophesied by the Lord Jesus with the words, *"Iniquity shall abound"* (Matthew 24:12). Luther translates this, "Unrighteousness shall overwhelm." We do not want to go into detail, but everyone knows that there is a great number of false teachers and prophets who are deceiving many. As a result, genuine Christians who love the Lord with all of their hearts and stand unconditionally on the Word of God are being mocked, rejected and laughed at.

The Earth Shall Reel As A Drunkard

There has always been violence, terror, war, rumors of war, disease, famine, earthquakes, storms, droughts, and floods, but they have never been so frequent as during this century. We have statistical proof that these types of so-called "natural catastrophes" are rapidly increasing. Literally millions of people are dying as a result of natural catastrophes each year. Our planet earth in its structure is experiencing movements which may have been known before, but not in the accelerated succession we are witnessing today. The often scientifically unexplainable increase of natural catastrophes is not limited to the geophysical earth and the climate pattern which surrounds the world, but also includes the structure of its societies with its governments. We can compare the world with an old car which is worn out and has become unpredictable in its function. Some 2,500 years ago, the prophet Isaiah predicted, *"The earth shall reel to and fro like a drunkard, and shall be removed like a cottage; and the transgression thereof shall be heavy upon it; and it shall fall, and not rise again"* (Isaiah 24:20).

The earth is indeed in a turmoil, and on the basis of these facts which have been confirmed over and again during the past few decades by scientists from around the world, fear among the population of the world is greatly increasing. More and more people, young and old alike, are in searching of an escape, and many are finding it in alcohol and drugs. As a result, we now have the highest rate of suicide in recorded history. Can we deny that we live in the time which was predicted by the Lord Jesus with the words, *"Men's hearts failing them for fear, and for looking after those things which are coming on the earth: for the powers of heaven shall be shaken"*? (Luke 21:26).

Growing Fear of a Nuclear Catastrophe

There is no exception; whether in the Western world or in the Communist world, the people and their respective governments live in fear of a nuclear war. In view of the threatening nuclear arsenals in the East and West, many ask, and rightly so, "What will happen in the future?" Although God permitted it, godless men have taken the world into their hands and are now capable of destroying it through nuclear energy.

Several decades ago it was scientifically unrealistic to talk about the terrible destruction that the Bible reported to us through the prophets. But in view of the latest discoveries, it has become very realistic. The most capable technicians and scientists are feverishly at work today to create even more terrible destructive weapons through which millions upon millions of people could be killed in a split second. A recently published report in Switzerland states:

America Remains Extremely Dangerous to the Soviet Union Even After a Nuclear Attack

The Soviet Union will not survive a nuclear war even if Moscow decides on a pre-emptive strike. The military strategists in Washington are planning with this theory in mind, with the support of the President of the United States, President Reagan.

The United States has cancelled 'first strike option'

in the use of nuclear weapons against the Soviet Union. Thus, the entire defense system is being built on the basis of a retaliatory strike against Russia. Military experts in America predict that a Soviet nuclear attack would result in an unprecedented disaster for the United States. However, that will not hinder a destructive, retaliatory strike by the United States. Two options are open:

1. Immediate nuclear attack after the Soviet Union's 'first strike.' This would result in less civil destruction because of the elaborate Soviet civil nuclear shelter system.

2. Reserve sufficient power to execute a second attack after the civilian population has returned from the nuclear shelters.

For this purpose, America is furthering the Trident system. The full capacity of this system will consist of 23 nuclear submarines of the 'Ohio' class. This type of nuclear submarine is, practically speaking, invincible due to its ability to withdraw to the depths of the oceans. The entire force of these nuclear submarines is capable of delivering a total of 500 Trident missiles, each containing 10 nuclear warheads. The strategy is obvious: Even if the USA is practically destroyed by a Soviet nuclear attack, America is still capable, even several months later, of destroying the Soviet Union. According to Pentagon estimates, more than 80% of Soviet industry would be destroyed. This retaliatory strike would cause a casualty figure of at least 140,000,000 people.

The greatest tragedy is that although most people

Israelis studying the Bible. From over 120 countries, Jews are returning to the Promised Land...

know the destructive power of nuclear weapons and realize that the majority of humanity could be killed in a relatively short time, they disregard that danger and make no preparation. Again, this has occurred before. It was the time before Noah's flood. *"For as in the days that were before the flood they were eating and drinking, marrying and giving in marriage, until the day that Noe entered into the ark, And knew not until the flood came, and took them all away; so shall also the coming of the Son of man be"* (Matthew 24:38,39).

The almost unlimited nuclear arms race is not only there to achieve a balance of power, but the very presence of these weapons forces them to be used. One day, when one least expects it, the spark of war will be ignited; it will be the world's first full-fledged nuclear war. In Revelation 9:15 we are told that one-third of mankind will be killed. The Apostle Peter saw this in his prophetic view and exclaimed, *"The end of all things is at hand"* (I Peter 4:7). The very things our world leaders and scientists fear were predicted by this simple fisherman, Peter, some 2,000 years ago. Old Bible scholars of the last centuries stated that "Peter is speaking about something we know nothing of." Indeed, fifty years ago, scientifically, it was utter nonsense. But today the world is trembling at the thought that it could be fulfilled: *"But the day of the Lord will come as a thief in the night; in the which the heavens shall pass away with a great noise, and the elements shall melt with fervent heat, the earth also and*

Israel's desert is literally blooming again precisely to the prediction of the Prophetic Word.

the works that are therein shall be burned up" (II Peter
3:10). Of this horrible happening, the Apostle John
also reports, for he, too, was a disciple of Jesus Christ
as was Peter. *"And I beheld when he had opened the
sixth seal, and, lo, there was a great earthquake; and the
sun became black as sackcloth of hair, and the moon
became as blood; And the stars of heaven fell unto the
earth, even as a fig tree casteth her untimely figs, when
she is shaken of a mighty wind. And the heaven
departed as a scroll when it is rolled together; and every
mountain and island were moved out of their places.
And the kings of the earth, and the great men, and the
rich men, and the chief captains, and the mighty men,
and every bondman, and every free man, hid themselves
in the dens and in the rocks of the mountains; And said
to the mountains and rocks, Fall on us, and hide us
from the face of him that sitteth on the throne, and from
the wrath of the Lamb: For the great day of his wrath is
come; and who shall be able to stand?"* (Revelation 6:12-
17).

We Are Living in a Dying World

This is indeed true whether we realize it or not.
Threatening clouds of judgment are seen rising in the
political world. It is much later than most people
think. Once the disciples asked their Master, *"Tell us,
when shall these things be? and what shall be the sign of
thy coming, and of the end of the world?"* (Matthew
24:3). Jesus answered them, *"Take heed that no man*

deceive you. For many shall come in my name, saying, I am Christ; and shall deceive many. And ye shall hear of wars and rumors of wars: see that ye be not troubled: for all these things must come to pass, but the end is not yet. For nation shall rise against nation, and kingdom against kingdom: and there shall be famines, and pestilences, and earthquakes, in divers places" (verses 4-7). The world has never experienced such horrible and bloody wars as it did in the last two world wars—it occurred in our century! Today it seems rather obvious that mankind stands before the third world war. Eisenhower once uttered a remarkable statement, "Without a spiritual rebirth of humanity, the earth cannot spare itself from its 'Calvary' of the third world war."

A very plain and visible sign of the approaching end is the natural catastrophes, as we have already seen. They are increasing rapidly around the earth.

Another important item the Bible speaks about concerning the end-time is the sign concerning the believer: *"Now the Spirit speaketh expressly, that in the latter times some shall depart from the faith, giving heed to seducing spirits, and doctrines of devils"* (I Timothy 4:1). There is no doubt that apostasy has established itself well in our churches. Why? Because of man's giving heed to seducing spirits and doctrines of devils. Many refuse to believe the Bible for what it says. Therefore, the reinterpretation of the Word of God has led to the place where people do not know any longer what the Bible really says. This can be seen especially in the visible sign, the only sign given to the Church, Israel. How many seducing spirits and false doctrines are disregarding the very plain teaching of the Bible regarding the nation Israel? But, this very sign, Israel, of which we spoke at the beginning of this book, is the timeclock of God. We have experienced that miracle; only three years after the Nazi regime murdered 6,000,000 Jews, the State of Israel was founded on May 14, 1948. This last return of the Jews to their homeland, Israel, is not a self-invented, political solution of some Jews, but it was foretold in the prophetic Scriptures thousands of years ago.

Because this event, the return of the Jews to their own country is now in progress, we know that the signs of the time for the end of the world are here today, visibly. These signs also herald the return of the Lord and, therewith, the end of the time of grace. The clock of history is standing shortly before midnight. What will happen then? The voice of the archangel will be heard, and the Rapture of the Church of Jesus will take place. That is what the Bible calls a "mystery." Paul says, *"Behold, I shew you a mystery"* (I Corinthians 5:51). Afterwards, the heavens will be opened, and the sign of the Son of man will appear visible for all the world. I deal with this subject in detail in my book, *The Rapture and Its Mystery*.

The World's Virtue is Approaching Its End

Not only time but also *"the fashion* [virtue] *of this world passeth away"* (I Corinthians 7:31). This means that as far as human society is concerned it will also pass away. In contrast to these negative facts which indicate that all things will pass away, the Scripture admonishes us in a triumphant way that Jesus Christ *"hath abolished death, and hath brought life and immortality to light through the gospel"* (II Timothy 1:10). What a wonderful statement and what a contrast to all other systems, may it be Communism or Socialism, liberalism or Capitalism. In religion, too, may it be cult or false teachings, all will be done away with. For that very reason the Bible warns all children of God not to be like-minded with the world, *"Love not the world, neither the things that are in the world. If any man love the world, the love of the Father is not in him. For all that is in the world, the lust of the flesh, and the lust of the eyes, and the pride of life, is not of the Father, but is of the world. And the world passeth away, and the lust thereof: but he that doeth the will of God abideth for ever. Little children, it is the last time: and as ye have heard that antichrist shall come, even now are there many antichrists; whereby we know that it is the last time"* (I John 2:15-18). How are we to understand, *"Even now are there many antichrists?"* Answer: The "antichrist" will not only be a person but also a collective and all-embracing system.

Antichrists for a Time

Indeed there always have been antichrists, but during the end of the end-time, this Antichrist will climax in world rulership and will be revealed as the "mystery of lawlessness." This is not something far into the future, but its beginning is much sooner than most dare to think. It is already history as far as his spirit is concerned. The Apostle Paul, inspired by the Holy Spirit, writes, *"For the mystery of iniquity doth already work"* (II Thessalonians 2:7). He then continues and says, *"Only he who now letteth will let, until he be taken out of the way. And then shall that Wicked be revealed."* Here we have the secret of the hindering element which is responsible for the delay of the full unfolding of the evil. It is the Church of Jesus Christ wherein dwelleth the Holy Spirit of God.

Even in the early Church, at the beginning, the antichristian spirit was at work. The Christian Church started in Jerusalem, and its members were exclusively Jews, of the stock of Israel. After the transfer was accomplished (the Messianic believing Jews passing it on to the heathens), God did indeed withdraw His hand from Israel. The Jewish people were dispersed across the face of the earth. After the death of the Jewish Apostles and the dispersion of the nation of Israel, the Gentile Christians lacked the spiritual leadership of the Jews from Israel. That was the reason the antichristian spirit could quickly get a foothold within the Church and establish its destruc-

Millions of people are becoming refugees in many parts of the world. Shown here: Refugees entering Cameroun.

tive false teachings among the members. Here we see the beginning of the establishment of the Antichrist and his teachings. Paul prophesied of this in Acts 20:29, *"For I know this, that after my departing shall grievous wolves enter in among you, not sparing the flock."* The Apostle John also testified about it, *"And every spirit that confesseth not that Jesus Christ is come in the flesh is not of God: and this is that spirit of antichrist, whereof ye have heard that it should come; and even now already is it in the world"* (I John 4:3). Once I read a fitting word in this regard, "Every dispensation has its own antichrist."

It is important to understand that the most dangerous enemies of Christianity do not come from outside powers. The greatest enemies of the Church of

Afghans escaping to Pakistan.

Jesus Christ are members of the Church who want to glorify their own flesh and refuse to be crucified with Christ and, therewith, stubbornly refuse to allow the Holy Spirit to work in their lives. How much argument has taken place in church history to this day! Many things written plainly in the Bible were twisted, reinterpreted and presented on a human level. How often have we Christians fought each other with highly exalted speeches. How often have we used our own selfishly established doctrine above the Word of God and above the commandment, "Love ye one another." This type of self-righteousness will be rebuked when the Lord comes to judge His saints. Such things within the Church belong to the "virtue of the world," or as the KJV translation says, *"the fashion of this world"* (I Corinthians 7:31). It does not belong in the fellowship of children of God. We need to cleanse ourselves and refuse to participate in these deeds. It is essential that it is done away with before the Rapture, which could happen at any time. Paul very strongly admonishes the believers with threatening words, *"But if ye bite and devour one another, take heed that ye be not consumed one of another"* (Galatians 5:15).

The Beginning of the End

The believer can clearly recognize the clouds of judgment on the horizon. Society is being pre-programmed so that the individual believes that he is entitled to have whatever he wants here and now; hence he occupies himself with things of the world—everything that is for his own advantage. While the Bible teaches to consider others, Satan answers, "Look out for yourself." That is a sign of the beginning of hell which is to come. Let us see this more clearly. People who think normal are being forced to think differently. For example, human rights policies have been placed in high priority in many countries, yet the result is that selfishness is increasing rapidly. Certainly we can compare our time to the time of Noah. On the one hand we see a brutal suppression of the pure faith in Jesus Christ, especially in the Eastern countries, and on the other hand in the Western world the Word of God is being presented on an attractive, emotional level to such an extent that even children of God are often unable to differentiate between the true Gospel and the imitation. We cannot deny that the world today respects religion, but it does so not for religious purposes but only for the furtherance of the materialistic mind. These types of temptations for children of God present the highest spiritual danger, because these materialistic, end-time tendencies belong to the sign of the beast. It is developing today in a very special way through the thinking and actions of men. We can summarize the sign of the Antichrist with one sentence: "Peace, peace, we demand our rights." This is the shout of the masses which throngs ahead but leaves behind a trail of blood and even fosters unrighteousness. There are no better words found in the Gospel exposing the political tendency and the "fashions of the world" today than the Word of our Lord, *"Because iniquity* [unrighteousness] *shall abound, the love of many shall wax cold"* (Matthew 24:12). Indeed, we have many peace movements today. Respectable citizens, the highly educated and intelligent participate, too, but the deepest motive is not peace but hate against the establishment, against anything that does not satisfy their own selfish desires. It is in exact opposition to the admonitions of the Apostle Paul, *"Let every soul be subject unto the higher powers. For there is no power but of God: the powers that be are ordained of God"* (Romans 13:1). The spirit of hate is rampant today but cleverly attempts to camouflage itself behind peace, religion, human rights, equal rights, etc. Yes, the words of the Lord Jesus are being fulfilled today; love is growing cold in many!

Legalism is included in this prophesied iniquity or unrighteousness. Legal forms and systems are brought about to suppress certain people, to bring them into great need, while others receive aid and preference legally. Persons who honestly report their income, for example, are being burdened with excessive taxes while many, who in reality are too lazy to work, are being rewarded by the State through this tax money. Indeed, unrighteousness shall increase! This type of systematic legalism is often the cause of violence and brutality among citizens. These symptoms which are common in all countries of the world are certainly repulsive and horrible, yet they are only the result of the beginning work of the antichristian spirit. The climax of this work will be the work of the Antichrist himself. At this time he cannot reveal himself because the light of the earth and the salt of the earth is still present, that is, the Church of Jesus Christ. But we ask, "How horrible will it be when the Church is taken away and the Antichrist will be revealed in person?" Christ describes this time with the words, *"For then shall be great tribulation, such as was not since the beginning of the world to this time, no, nor ever shall be"* (Matthew 24:21).

Judgment Over the Nations

The second phase of the Second Coming of the Son of God will result, first of all, in the cleansing of the demonized atmosphere of the world. We know that the first phase of the Second Coming will be the Rapture, when the Lord will meet us in the air. He will not come to earth. In the second phase of the Second Coming, He will physically come on the earth and His feet will stand on the Mount of Olives (Zechariah 14:4). What will happen when Christ will be revealed visibly as the victor over the Antichrist? Everything which is not of the Son of God will be exposed, notably all of the religious societies, which fundamentally speaking, are antichristian in character. There are false prophets just as the Son of God has prophesied, because they do not accept the only way of salvation but further self-redemption. All will be exposed when facing the truth. All self-made religions do not teach things pertaining to God but are centered around self. One of those religions which is flooding the world triumphantly today is Islam, whose prophet Mohammed is often called the false prophet. Some scholars even prefer to identify him as the antichrist of the east.

Although Mohammed recognized the true God and testified of the God of Israel, he claimed to be the highest representative and the true prophet. His claim centered on his self-revelation; thus we know he was a false representative of a false god. From reading our Bible and comparing the statements of Mohammed, we clearly recognize that he was unable to legitimatize himself through signs and miracles as the true ambassador of the Most High God. Instead of supernatural signs inspired by the Holy Spirit, he had to use an opposing tool, that is, *fire* and *sword*. Hence, it became a religion of force. Because blood always calls for blood, it produced fanatical disciples who forcefully propagated this new religion with tremendous success. This religion without love flooded quickly the borders of the Mideast into Asia, North Africa and parts of southern Europe.

For many centuries the population of Europe, who represented Christianity, was threatened by Islamic nations. This religion is an abomination unto the Lord not only because of the demonic force integrated into the religion but because they deny the Son of God. As a result of this religion, which is without love and based on brutal force, the nations whose religion is Islam are suffering today. But they, too, will be redeemed from this false religious oppression by the Son of God when He will make an end of all imitations in the battle of Armageddon.

The Thousand Years
Kingdom of Peace

Only after everything which is counterfeit, unreal, and does not comply with the Truth (who has now appeared in person) has been done away with, will the thousand years reign of peace by the King of all kings begin. This coming visible peace on earth is well documented in our Bible and consists of two parts: First, the destruction of the evil, *"And cast him into the bottomless pit, and shut him up, and set a seal upon him.* Second, the result of the imprisonment or neutralization of the evil, *"That he should deceive the nations no more, till the thousand years be fulfilled: and after that he must be loosed a little season"* (Revelation 20:3). The thousand years kingdom of peace is a wonderful reality and is the final answer of Jesus' prayer, *"Thy kingdom come. Thy will be done in earth, as it is in heaven"* (Matthew 6:10). I have written on this subject in detail in my book, *Thousand Years Peace: A Utopia?*

Inevitable Judgment

Some readers may ask the question, "Can I still be saved during the Great Tribulation?" The Bible does not give an answer whether *you* can be saved during the Great Tribulation. While you read this book you have a chance right now to come to the Lord as you are, because the promise is valid, "He who cometh to me I will in no wise cast out" (John 6:37). The Bible does say, however, that during the Great Tribulation, scores of people will be saved, but with utmost difficulty, because then they will lose their life by force.

Today, however, while the Church of Jesus Christ is still present on earth, there is still the open door of grace, and you may come to the Lord Jesus just as you are and need not go through the Great Tribulation.

At the end of the Great Tribulation, the peace kingdom of Christ will begin. After that, time will be no more; eternity has begun. But eternity can start for you today. It could start for millions of people in one day when the nuclear catastrophe will take place on this planet. But not only the threat of a nuclear war stands at our door, there are other terrible events about to explode in a climax. As an example, here is a quote from the book *Wenn Die Erde Kippt* by G. von Hassler:

> There doesn't seem to be much difference for the casualty whether he be destroyed by a nuclear bomb, nerve gas, or a rifle bullet. But it makes a great difference to know that the Western world is in actual fact supporting with its own technology, science, money, weapons, the Communist ideologies of the East. Thus, the West is supplying the rope to its executioners.
>
> No one less than Lenin himself predicted with his instinctively sharp political analysis, even without the assistance of computers, the behavior of those whose god is the consumer product. In his writing, Lenin predicted the victory of Communism over capitalism back in 1921 with the words, 'They will supply us with the needed materials and the technologies which we lack. They will also assist us in building our arms industry which we will use in our victorious attack against the suppliers.' In other words, the West will work hard to supply the East with weapons for their own destruction. At this very

moment, we have not quite reached that point, but we are certainly aiming at that direction. We can only hope that the coming catastrophe of the third world war with its accompanying nuclear threat will not occur before 1985.

Resurrection For All

I may be overemphasizing it, but I must repeat: there is no way out. Judgment will even come for those who have committed suicide. The end is not by taking one's own life. The end to everything is not for those who had their body cremated either, thinking to be gone once and for all. We have undisputable proof in the Word of God that everyone will be raised from the dead, *"And I saw a great white throne, and him that sat on it, from whose face the earth and the heaven fled away; and there was found no place for them. And I saw the dead, small and great, stand before God; and the books were opened: and another book was opened, which is the book of life: and the dead were judged out of those things which were written in the books, according to their works. And the sea gave up the dead which were in it; and death and hell delivered up the dead which were in them: and they were judged every man according to their works. And death and hell were cast into the lake of fire. This is the second death. And whosoever was not found written in the book of life was cast into the lake of fire"* (Revelation 20:11-15).

Every human being who has ever lived will be resurrected whether he wants to or not. The Bible tells us that it will be so. In the book of the prophet Daniel we read, *"And many of them that sleep in the dust of the earth shall awake, some to everlasting life, and some to shame and everlasting contempt"* (Daniel 12:2). Christ Himself, over whose lips no untruth ever came and no imperfect word was ever uttered, stated, *"Marvel not at this: for the hour is coming, in the which all that are in the graves shall hear his voice, And shall come forth; they that have done good, unto the resurrection of life; and they that have done evil, unto the resurrection of damnation"* (John 5:28,29). Paul the Apostle testifies of this fact, too, and states that without exception all will be brought back to life, *"For as in Adam all die, even so in Christ shall all be made alive. But every man in his own order: Christ the firstfruits; afterward they that are Christ's at his coming. Then cometh the end, when he shall have delivered up the kingdom to God, even the Father; when he shall have put down all rule and all authority and power. For he must reign, till he hath put all enemies under his feet"* (I Corinthians 15:22-25). This will be the final fulfillment of Easter. The power of the resurrection of Jesus Christ will be extended to the utmost borders. No man, no deed, no word can be hidden then. Everything will be revealed before the Father and the Lord Jesus Christ.

There is No Escape

Dear friend, this book was not written for the purpose of entertainment. I must warn you on the basis of the Holy Scripture that there is no way out. Do not be so foolish as to think that you can withdraw yourself from the last judgment! We read in the Bible that heaven and earth shall try to flee from the face of Him who sitteth upon the throne. How horrible it will be for all those who now reject the only offer of true salvation. Back in the beginning of history at the time of creation, Adam and Eve sinned and subsequently attempted to hide themselves from the judging countenance of God. But they could not. They were unsuccessful. God did see them. In Paradise, they found a place to hide, although they could not hide from God. The Bible clearly emphasizes that at the Last Judgment all places of hiding, every item of comouflaging, will be done away with. The expression, "earth and heaven" is not a common expression we find in the Bible. It shows to us that God is now dealing exclusively with man. The entire universe, the never-ending space, is no hiding place for man either. All of it will tremble before the face of God. Now man stands uncovered and exposed before the living God, whom he has rejected. Everything is now revealed, may it be your profession, family, marriage, culture, your entire life. But everything else is done away with. Only you stand by yourself before a judging God.

The end of the world, or to be precise, the end of God's creation, serves now to reveal man's true state. Now, he cannot hide behind the Antichrist, or Satan, or his theory of the universe and his scientific knowledge. He stands alone before God. Let us re-read this sentence for it says literally, *"From whose face the earth and the heaven fled away; and there was found no place for them"* (Revelation 20:11). This means the entire creation does not flee somewhere, but it flees into nowhere. When God makes something disappear, it does disappear and man, who may have placed his entire hope on nature, has now become hopeless.

You Will Stand Before God

Now the stage is set and there is, practically speaking, total emptiness except man and his God. When we talk about God we understand that the Lamb, the Church of Jesus and the angels are included. But everything else with which man has occupied himself so much on earth, his philosophies and his self-created theologies are gone. Men now stand without support before God: man and his Creator. There is no more dispute about it. We see it in our Bible. It is written, *"And I saw the dead, small and great, stand before God."* I am sure that these people standing before God would like to escape. They would like to flee from Him who sitteth upon the throne. But now, there is no escape. All is done away with. Now everyone MUST stand before God. Now, however, He is no longer the loving God, the gracious Saviour, but now He is the Judge. While everything is being dissolved into nothing, man remains. Man will see and experience that everything will be done away with.

He even may have wished that he was done away with in death, because now the truth is being revealed about him. There is no way of escaping from the Creator, neither through suicide nor through cremation. Death is not the finality of life, but the beginning of eternity. God Himself has reserved the final act. He is the Alpha and Omega. He is the First and the Last.

Everyone Will Be Revealed Before God

There is one more thing which needs to be mentioned. While man stands before God, unable to escape because there is no escape, he stands before Him regardless of his position. Class distinction is done away with, too. We clearly read, *"I saw the dead, small AND great, stand before God."* Thus, this is not only an individual judgment, but it is also a collective judgment. Of course, every single person will be judged individually; that is true. But at the same time, every person will be judged in the presence of all others. Everyone will be revealed before God in front of all. Hence the final judgment for the individual will also be the judgment of all.

With this last resurrection of the individual, the completion of the resurrection power of Jesus has come. Easter is indeed a one-time occurrence, but the result of Easter continues irresistibly. From the first resurrection, to the second, the general resurrection, it continues until it has reached every single individual of all of mankind from its very beginning to its very end. I must repeat NO ONE, absolutely no one, can escape from Jesus. No one can be neutral regarding the person Jesus. This is because the resurrection of Jesus Christ is more than only His resurrection, which was a world-shaking and tremendous event, but His resurrection power will continue to work until everyone is resurrected. Therefore, whoever denies the resurrection of Jesus subsequently denies the last resurrection, too. Everything is synchronized with the resurrection of Jesus. It is the same way with death; it does not make exception, it meets every individual, rich or poor, old or young, small or great. Death is a reality and an opposing factor against God; thus God's plan of redemption is also a reality in opposition to death. It certainly would be an imperfect victory if death would have stopped at a certain group of people. As a result, the victory of Jesus would not need to be effective with them. Then the Gospel would not be a gospel and the message of salvation would not mean what it says. Especially in regard to death, we realize fully the message of victory we have in the Lord Jesus Christ. Death is the most brutal opposition to the living God, but it will end. Because Jesus is the victor, He has in reality defeated all His enemies perfectly and absolutely! Especially during this second resurrection of eternal judgment, His victory over hell, death and the devil is demonstrated in a unique way. If there is a voice to be heard during this last judgment, then it will be the voice of Him who sitteth upon the throne and no one else!

The Great Silence

Of those who are being judged we hear nothing, but it simply says they *"stand before God."* They have nothing to say anymore. They don't answer, dispute or argue because now everything is revealed and they are not being asked. Repeatedly, we read in Revelation that the judgment is taking place in accordance with that which is written. No answer can help anymore. Only that which is written is decisive. Man stands before his Creator and he is being judged not in the manner as it is done in our courts where mistakes can be made and somehow the accused can be freed. I am convinced that there are many who have thought well about what they will answer, how they will excuse themselves, but let it be said: there will be no answer! No explanation need be made. Everything, absolutely everything, is revealed. And on the basis of those facts which are written in God's book, judgment will take place.

Better to End in Fear
Than to Fear Without End

To describe the last part of this judgment is practically speaking impossible. It is so difficult and so terrible because there is no end. It is plainly said, *"And whosoever was not found written in the book of life was cast into the lake of fire"* (Revelation 20:15). That is the true Hell, the most horrible place anyone can think of. It is described for us in detail with the words, *"And he shall be tormented with fire and brimstone in the presence of the holy angels, and in the presence of the Lamb: And the smoke of their torment ascendeth up for ever and ever: and they have no rest day nor night"* (Revelation 14:10,11).

These facts do not change with your philosophy or your understanding of theology. It makes absolutely no difference whether you believe it or not. It will, nevertheless, happen just exactly in the way it is written. There is only one positive note in it. Today, you can be saved from this horrible place of torment which is approaching you. As a matter of fact, Jesus, who rose from the dead, is actually waiting for you today. But you do not have much time. The Bible says in Psalm 102:11, *"My days are like a shadow that declineth; and I am withered like grass."* You may not realize it when you are young, but you will notice it quickly when you get older. Yet age makes in reality no difference, for you do not know if today you may be killed in a car accident or tomorrow you may get ill and die. Do you know what comes after death? Eternity! Thus, in this regard too, you do not have much time, because you do not know when your time will be up.

In the world of nations, that is in the political world, we see the action of the Lord very clearly. Why?

Test of a Trident missile, capable of accurately delivering ten nuclear warheads, each being 15 times the size of those dropped on Hiroshima.

Because the time is very near when Christ will return again. Bible prophecy is being fulfilled before our eyes in rapid succession as never before. Events predicted thousands of years ago are being fulfilled today. In the last few decades, a great many prophetic statements have been fulfilled or are progressively being fulfilled. Who would have thought only four decades ago that the Jews would be able to return to the country promised to them by God and establish their own state? Not to mention the fact that the State of Israel with its immense and unique difficulties is, in actual fact, a miracle itself from any point of view. This natural rebirth of Israel is only the beginning, because spiritual renewal will follow and is already in the process of beginning. Very exactly, the Lord's prophecy through Isaiah is being fulfilled, *"I the Lord will hasten it in his time"* (Isaiah 60:22).

People who are saved, although they may die before the Lord comes, are, nevertheless, eternal people. If you are still not saved today, then let it be known now, there is not much time to prepare for eternity. But the good news is that preparation can be made today. You don't have to stand in line to wait. You don't have to fill out application forms. You only need to come to Him who promised, *"Him that cometh to me I will in no wise cast out"* (John 6:37). The most important thing in all of your life is to have forgiveness of sins or else you stand before God's countenance in judgment. The Lord Jesus has shed His own precious and holy blood for you. He has purchased you and with it paid for your sins. Permit His words to be fulfilled through you personally, *"He that overcometh, the same shall be clothed in white raiment; and I will not blot out his name out of the book of life, but I will confess his name before my Father, and before his angels"* (Revelation 3:5). It is impossible for you to cleanse yourself and only with a spotless heart will you be able to stand before God. Even more, you will spend timeless eternity with God. That has also been prophesied by the Lord, *"Blessed are the pure in heart: for they shall see God"* (Matthew 5:8). In the heavenly world to come, the place of utter glory, there is no room for sin. This is emhasized very clearly in the last book of the Bible, *"And there shall in no wise enter into it any thing that defileth, neither whatsoever worketh abomination, or maketh a lie: but they which are written in the Lamb's book of life"* (Revelation 21:27).

Are You Ready to Meet the Eternal God?

Maybe you confess to be a Christian because you belong to a church. You are baptized. You may be confirmed. You may even be actively involved in your church. Whoever you are and whatever your position is now, it is important to realize that when the time comes and you stand before the great throne of God, you will not be able to use any kind of defense for yourself, because God is righteous and His very righteousness will reveal your very true nature. We have seen that the books will be opened and those books are heavenly books. There is no room for errors. That book shows that your name has been blotted out because you have rejected God's eternal gift of salvation which He has offered you through the sacrifice of His own Son. There will be no question asked. You will not even be able to point to others who may have misused the Gospel. Only one question is decisive: what have you done with the Son of God, Jesus Christ?

There is no one who is able to tell you how long you may live. Maybe today is your last day. No one knows, and you don't know if tomorrow you will still be alive. For that reason, the Lord so decidedly says, *"Today if ye will hear his voice, harden not your hearts"* (Hebrews 4:7). Even if everything seems to be hopeless for you, if you are deeply disappointed and you already sense the clouds of desperation above you, which may seem to indicate that your life is useless, there is still a tremendous possibility. Millions have experienced it before. There *is* new life in Jesus. Therefore, confess unto Him today, "Lord Jesus, I come to you the way I am. I seek cleansing from my sins and salvation through your blood. I want to belong to you for all of eternity!" The Word of God guarantees that He will accept you, and He will make your life new, too.

Chapter Two

The Vertical and Horizontal End-Time Events

This may seem to be a rather strange title, but it is very significant as we will see in this chapter when we compare God's events and man's events. Again, we emphasize that we view the entire world in its approaching end, because God is about to create something totally new.

The times we live in are marked by events occurring in such rapid succession as never experienced before. But this is also a wonderful time for which we should thank the Almighty, because in our generation, we have become eyewitnesses of God's visible action in world history. In actual fact, we are seeing with our eyes and hearing with our ears the things our forefathers desired to see and hear. From Christian literature dating back only one century, we realize that there were some of our forefathers who desired the things we are seeing. We are experiencing today events which they could see only in faith, namely, the preparation for the return of Jesus Christ and the restoration of the kingdom of God on earth. We are seeing the restoration of Israel!

Psalm 2 talks about the horizontal and the vertical events. The horizontal is that which man does. It includes world politics and world history. The vertical are the actions of God. They are God's deeds from heaven down to earth. *"Why do the heathen rage, and the people imagine a vain thing? The kings of the earth set themselves, and the rulers take counsel together, against the Lord, and against his anointed, saying, Let us break their bands asunder, and cast away their cords from us"* (Psalm 2:1-3). These are horizontal events. *"He that sitteth in the heavens shall laugh: the Lord shall have them in derision. Then shall he speak unto them in his wrath, and vex them in his sore displeasure. Yet have I set my king upon my holy hill of Zion. I will declare the decree: the Lord hath said unto me, Thou art my Son; this day have I begotten thee. Ask of me, and I shall give thee the heathen for thine inheritance, and the uttermost parts of the earth for thy possession"* (verses 4-8). These are vertical events; God's actions from heaven are in opposition to the dealings of man.

The center of all horizontal events, as well as vertical events, is a person, the person Jesus Christ. When He, the Son of God, was born in the fullness of time, God completed His greatest vertical act, *"God was in Christ, reconciling the world unto himself"* (II Corinthians 5:19). That was the unfathomable, eternally valid event of all time. God indeed *"obtained eternal redemption for us"* (Hebrews 9:12). The finished work of His first coming on earth was the crucifixion of the Son of God. Jesus Christ, the bearer of sin, was hanging between heaven and earth on the cross of Calvary. He, in actual fact, carried away the sins of the world and reconciled man with God. That is the reason why the very educated, highly intelligent Apostle Paul wrote to the Corinthians, *"For I determined not to know anything among you, save Jesus Christ, and him crucified"* (I Corinthians 2:2). We can actually say that through God's vertical action He crossed out man's intention and man's way of destruction which are initiated by His enemy, Satan. When speaking about the horizontal and the vertical end-time events, then we are speaking about Jesus Christ the soon returning world ruler, for He is the center of both. His first coming and His return make up the vertical line. The Bible teaches very clearly that He will come to Israel, to be precise in Jerusalem, visible for all men, *"And his feet shall stand in that day upon the mount of Olives, which is before Jerusalem on the east"* (Zechariah 14:4). Because of this vertical action of God, we see today the horizontal actions of the world opposing it. It is rather fascinating to see that this city, Jerusalem, and the people, Israel, are being put into the spotlight of the world increasingly. Thus the vertical end-time sign is manifesting itself through the nation of Israel with their capital city, Jerusalem, and through the Church of Jesus Christ on earth. These facts cannot be changed, in spite of the world's political movements and the leaders with all of their conferences and negotiation. The vertical events oppose the horizontal events. Through the small nation Israel and invisibly through the Church, God is intervening in the plans and intentions of the nations of the world.

View to Calvary

Whoever views the Crucified One begins to recognize the original conflict between the Holy God and sinful man. Here one begins to see the triumphant solution God has achieved. Calvary is the bridge between God's holiness and His love. Our eternal God and Creator is holy and righteous. No sinner can possibly stand before Him. There is absolutely no exception. Every man is a sinner from his birth. This is confirmed in the Bible, *"There is none righteous, no, not one"* (Romans 3:10). On the other hand, the holy Scripture clearly teaches that God is also love (I John 4:8). On the basis of His love, He found a way to pay for the sin of man and reconcile Himself with a lost humanity in a very unique way, *"For God so loved the world, that he gave his only begotten Son, that whosoever believeth in him should not perish, but have everlasting life"* (John 3:16). With this vertical deed God intervened into man's horizontal ways. He crossed out and He destroyed man's plan and aim which can only lead to death. The plan God has for Israel, He also has for each individual person. He wants you to live for eternity. This eternal life God gave to His Son Jesus Christ, who cried out when dying on the cross, *"It is finished"* (John 19:30), can be yours. With that deed, God solved the conflict between light and darkness. For the second time, God divided light from the darkness, as He already did in the beginning. When He created the world He said, *"And God said, Let there be light: and there was light. And God saw the light, that it was good: and God divided the light from the darkness"* (Genesis 1:3,4).

However, the separation between light and darkness has not reached its finality yet. Of course, it has already been decided: Christ is the victor. He defeated the power of darkness once and for all on the cross of Calvary. That was the beginning of the end of Satan. But now this victory must be visibly demonstrated before the whole world. That is the actual reason why there is such a terrible and tremendously great battle going on today in the spiritual realm. All the events about which we may hear in our news media are the visible results of nothing other than the bitter and hostile protest of hate against the vertical aims of God.

Karl Marx, the father of Communism, wrote in one of his poems, "I desire to take revenge against Him who rules above." That statement proves that he was convinced of the existence of heaven and the supreme God who rules. Karl Marx's statements are also proof of the spiritual battle between man's horizontal line and God's vertical line. Today, too, we have millions upon millions of people who really hate God. Outwardly, they deny the existence of God. But inwardly, deep down in their hearts, they know about Him. That is the exact reason why they so vehemently oppose Christians. In our time it is expressed especially in the hate toward Israel and Jerusalem, because Israel and its people are a visible proof of the existence of God. It is no surprise, therefore, that Communist countries hate Israel, because the very existence of that nation is proof that their own invented theology which claims "God is dead" is false.

Israel:
The Center of End-Time Events

Israel's bare existence not only contradicts Communism but all other philosophies and ideologies, too. Daily, we hear in our news media something about Israel, may it be positive or negative. Israel's position is a repetition of that which happened to one person, the person Jesus Christ, the Son of God and the Son of Israel. He is in the center of these two lines, in the center between God and man, between light and darkness. There is something miraculous about this nation, and the whole world agrees, but, because Israel contradicts the world in its philosophy, they must be rejected and isolated. Israel does not fit into the line of the political thinking of the world. Israel is standing between these two poles, between positive and negative, light and darkness, action of God and action of man. But because Jesus Christ the great Son of Israel lives, Israel will live, too. It is Jesus Christ who has brought about with His own precious blood the reconciliation between God and man on the cross of Calvary outside Jerusalem. The great enemy, the opposer of God, is defeated once and for all, but it is not visible to the entire world yet. As believers we are part of Israel, as is plainly documented for us in the book of Ephesians, *"That at that time ye were without Christ, being aliens from the commonwealth of Israel, and strangers from the covenants of promise, having no hope, and without God in the world: But now in Christ Jesus ye who sometimes were far off are made nigh by the blood of Christ. For he is our peace, who hath made both one, and hath broken down the middle wall of partition between us; Having abolished in his flesh the enmity, even the law of commandments contained in ordinances; for to make in himself of twain one new man, so making peace; And that he might reconcile both unto God in one body by the cross, having slain the enmity thereby"* (Ephesians 2:12-16). We can call this the "mystery of Calvary," which we can never fully comprehend in its depth with our intellect. Only our full comprehension of the vertical line enables us to realize that the horizontal line of the world must reject God's covenant people. And indeed today they are doing it more and more.

Israel:
The Sign of the Coming King

The nations of the world wish to do away with this

sign, which is given to us in our days, whether they do it consciously as the Communists do, or unconsciously as the rest of the world does. It is certainly not the desire of the world to see Israel being placed in the center more and more. Thus we can ask with the Psalmist the question, *"Why do the heathen rage, and the people imagine a vain thing?"* (Psalm 2:1). If the nations of the world would ask that question, they would begin to realize what they are doing. As a result they would begin to support Israel wholeheartedly, because then they would see that God will fulfill His plan regardless of their intention. In actual fact, whoever fights against Israel, fights against God! This statement is true for the believer, too. There are many Christians who deep down in their hearts harbor anti-Semitic thoughts against Israel. Such a one is not only an enemy of Israel but, indeed, he is an enemy of God, too. Just a look at recent history confirms this statement convincingly. All anti-Semites who fought against the Jews in the past have been put to shame and are destroyed. We can go as far back as the Roman times. Their destruction of Jerusalem did not satisfy them. They continud to persecute Jewish people, but today they are no more. The same goes for the Crusaders, the Turks, the Arabs, and Nazi Germany. Whoever attempts to fight the Jewish people attempts to eliminate the vertical line of which Israel is a part. Today's strongest body of anti-Semites is the United Nations which represents the entire world. But they,

Only three years after the end of the "final solution" of the Jewish question by Nazi Germany, David Ben-Gurion declares the founding of the State of Israel, May 14, 1948.

The arms race madness has not ceased since the establishment of Israel. Tests with chemical weapons being exercised by the Warsaw pact countries.

too, will experience the old statement which was made thousands of years ago to Israel. The word proclaimed in Egypt concerning Israel is being fulfilled again today, *"The more they afflicted them, the more they multiplied and grew"* (Exodus 1:12). The horrible attempts to destroy Israel before it became a nation, as was done by Pharaoh of Egypt who ordered every newborn Israelite boy to be thrown into the Nile, ended in the oppostie of his intention: Israel moved out of Egypt as a strong nation, free to serve God, but Pharaoh drowned. This same succession has repeated itself throughout the centuries. Every attempt to annihilate the Jewish people has failed, in spite of the fact that millions upon millions had to die. The end-result of the horrible murder of Jewish people before and during World War II was not the end of the Jews, but the opposite happened. It ended in the re-establishment of the State of Israel!

Today there is a difference, however. Before the founding of the State in 1948, there was one country persecuting and killing the Jews (Hitler's Germany). Today, many countries (almost all of the nations of the world) are expressing their desire to persecute one nation. We can indeed say that all nations of the world either are against Israel or are beginning to turn against Israel. Today, anti-Semitism is often camouflaged or hidden behind anti-Zionism which is, however, one and the same thing. We must not disregard the reports from many countries where it is statistically proven that anti-Semitic acts are increasing rapidly. While in Israel, I met a Dutch Jewess who has made it her habit to move from one city to another in Holland because of anti-Semitism. Quoting opinion polls in a number of countries a report said that 70% of Austrians are anti-Semitic, 50% in West Germany and Switzerland, and 30% in America. These people openly confess to be hostile to Jews. In 1981, there were 11,000 reported anti-Semitic acts throughout the Western world.

Anti-Semitic Hunters

Although it sounds very contradictory, the rapidly increasing worldwide anti-Semitic spirit will turn out for the good for Israel. From the Scripture we learn that this will be one of the tools to bring the Jews back home to their own country, the country promised to them by God. In the book of Jeremiah we read the prophecy, *"But, The Lord liveth, that brought up the children of Israel from the land of the north, and from all the lands whither he had driven them: and I will bring them again into their land that I gave unto their fathers. Behold, I will send for many fishers, saith the Lord, and they shall fish them; and after will I send for many hunters, and they shall hunt them from every mountain, and from every hill, and out of the holes of the rocks"* (Jeremiah 16:15,16). These are plain words. Many Jews will be forced back to Israel because of anti-Semitism, thus accelerating the events at the center of God's horizontal and vertical end-time signs.

The Jew Outside Israel

An open letter, by a Jew named Henryk Broder, published in Germany's press, addressed to the citizens of West Germany, contained a summary of anti-Zionism and the age-old anti-Semitism.

The Jew of today is the State of Israel. Just as your parents assumed that things would go better without the Jews, today you think things would go better without Israel, for then at least there would be no Mideast conflict. You are prepared to overlook the fact that there is not one Arab state in the Middle East that did not have a threatening conflict with another Arab state, yet you have made up your mind that Israel is the problem, the hindrance for peace and progress of socialism.

Who are those, I ask, who are so upset about Israel? Who oppose Israel's settlement policy? Who seem to see human rights violation on the West Bank? Who talk constantly about the disadvantaged Israeli Arabs? Do you know who they are? They are the same people who unhesitatingly accept Russia's invasion of Afghanistan. They are the people who don't even know that Tibet is occupied by China. They prefer to place Mr. Begin on the level of terrorists such as Idi Amin, Qadafi, or Khomeni. They are not interested at all that the Kurdish people are being systematically destroyed in Turkey. And they don't give a sound of protest about the hundreds of Kurds being killed every single day in Iran and Iraq. Would they oppose the genocide in Ethiopia today? Of course, they have not heard a thing about the openly practiced discrimination against gypsies in West Germany....

Henryk Broder knows the deep roots of this new type of anti-Semitism. He is frustrated that two measures are being used by the nations. Especially depressing is Christianity where anti-Semitism is being bred on a camouflaged level. Later, he reported:

'It's Christmas Eve.' I listen to WDR, (West German newscast). Headline news comes from Rome. 'Christians and Moslems are urged by Pope John Paul II to work toward unity for the liberation of Jerusalem.' The Holy City, it is asserted, must have free access by all religions. No one seems to think there is anything wrong with such a statement. Everyone simply ignores the fact that Jerusalem is liberated. There is free access to anyone of any religion since 1967. I do not wish to identify the moral qualities of the institution which is personalized by the Pope, but in humility I wish to call to remembrance that there was no official voice of protest heard from any Pope before 1967. He did not call for free access to the holy places. The reason was simple: all religions had access to their holy places except the Jews. Today, while Jerusalem is under the sovereignty of the Jews and permits all confessions to exercise their religious preference, the world in actual fact is calling for a 'free Jerusalem.' The worst thing in this matter, however, is that no one protests, no one opposes. Everyone simply accepts such irresponsible statements as normal.

With this statement of a Jew who decided to leave a free country to *the free country*, the home of his fathers, we have come to the center of the horizontal and vertical lines of end-time events, namely Jerusalem. This city is the heart of Israel and is called the residence of the Eternal. *"The LORD shall yet choose Jerusalem"* (Zechariah 1:17; cf. Zechariah 2:12 and 3:2). All of the protests we hear in the world regarding the so-called liberation of Jerusalem, which is interpreted today to mean internationalization of Jerusalem, is in opposition to the determined and precise aim God has for Jerusalem:

1. The re-establishment of the Kingdom of God on earth in Jerusalem.
2. The return of His Son to Jerusalem.
3. The blessed world rulership of the King of all kings from Jerusalem.

This city, Jerusalem, against which the entire world is turning today, is another proof of the truth of the Bible. God in His Word through the prophet Zechariah said, *"I will gather all nations against Jerusalem to battle"* (Zechariah 14:2). Opposition to Jerusalem is growing on the worldwide level and is fulfillment of prophecy. This will continue until it climaxes in the battle of Armageddon, when all the nations of the world will gather against Israel. Then Jesus Christ, the Messiah of Israel, will suddenly appear in great power and glory with His Church and make an end of the nations.

Jerusalem: The Cup of Trembling

Why, we may ask, do the nations oppose Jerusalem? Or an even more simple question, why do all the nations of the world refuse to place their embassies in the capital city of Israel? It, too, is fulfillment of Bible prophecy and it is of God for He Himself stated, *"I will make Jerusalem a cup of trembling unto all the people round about"* (Zechariah 12:2). The word "trembling" can also be translated with the word "poison" or "intoxicating." Thus the nations today are doing something against their own reason and logic. They are opposing Jerusalem because God has made them drink from His "cup of trembling." How else could we understand that, for instance, the United States of America, the only friend, or to be precise, "conditional, limited friend of Israel," bows to every demand of an undemocratic, dictatorial government like Saudi Arabia, which is a deadly enemy of Israel? Publicly, Saudi Arabia has announced its intentions to "liberate" Jerusalem. These intentions are fully supported through the action of the United States by supplying Saudi Arabia with the most sophisticated American war material which they don't need. We are purposely talking about America, because it is the only country who is still helping Israel, although with reservation. Why does the U.S.A. unhesitatingly help Israel's deadly enemies? Even Jordan, who agrees with the PLO to "liberate all of Palestine," is being considered by our foreign office to receive extremely offensive weapons! We need not to be experts to know that American-supplied weapons are only aimed at Israel. These and other events are the horizontal attacks upon Israel, because they are the center of the battlefield on the horizontal line.

Jerusalem: The Battlefield of the Vertical Line

But Israel is also the battlefield of the vertical line, that is, the spiritual. The reason for that is an historic fact because this city, the city of Jerusalem, has become God's special property and Satan, through the nations, has attempted repeatedly to take total possession of the city.

A believer who seeks God and walks through Israel can find the footprints of the Lord Jesus in this country. Nowhere in the world can one be so spiritually revived, receive courage for the disheartened and joy for new life than here, because this country has a great future. The great coming King is to rule the world from this place.

This country is not only the center of the geographical world, but also of the spiritual world. The good as well as the evil occurring in the world either originates or will climax in Israel. God's dealing with man, His plan of salvation, originated here and will also be completed here. Here was the place where the Spirit of God was poured upon the first believers and since then has enflamed millions around the world. Because the earth is round, the end will be met by the beginning. The river of blessings which issued from Jerusalem is about to come back to Jerusalem, its original source. Good and evil comes from Jerusalem and will go back to Jerusalem. And I must repeat, Israel is the strategic center of the battlefield of the Spirit because:

- Here the angels of light fought against the angels of darkness when Abraham moved into this country known at that time as Canaan. This same battle repeated itself when Israel moved into the Promised Land, redeemed from slavery in Egypt. This battle continued later between the false and the true prophets.
- Here the Son of God was born.
- Here He won the decisive victory.
- Here the Holy Spirit was poured upon the initiating group of believers giving birth to the Church of Jesus Christ.
- Because of Jerusalem the last battle of the Spirit will take place.
- Here the last battle, the battle of Armageddon, will take place, too.
- And here Christ will establish, after His Second Return, the millennial reign of peace on earth.

The Garden Tomb outside Jerusalem where the body of Christ was buried and where He arose on the third day.

God did not choose Moscow, Paris, London, or Washington, but He chose the small country Israel, with the capital city Jerusalem. This place is where He made His eternal decisions. For that reason, Satan also chooses Jerusalem as his capital of the world, and from here he, too, is directing his legions of demons in an attempt to oppose God's plans. In no other city in the world do we sense the reality of Ephesians 6:12 as we do in Jerusalem, *"For we wrestle not against flesh and blood, but against principalities, against powers, against the rulers of the darkness of this world, against spiritual wickedness in high places."*

We cannot see it with our physical eyes, but because God has chosen Jerusalem, Satan has a special interest in Jerusalem, too, and everyone who approaches the Holy Land, even the Holy City, is drawn into this spiritual conflict. One who has traveled many times to Israel knows that to be a fact. If one goes to Haifa (city in northern Israel), one feels a much quieter atmosphere spiritually and emotionally than in Jerusalem. The reason? *"For there* [Jerusalem] *are set thrones of judgments"* (Psalm 122:5).

The Separating Effects of Jerusalem

We can travel to Jerusalem with the best of intentions, but if the motive of our heart is not purified by the Spirit of God, then we can stand before the gates of Jerusalem, as once did the Crusaders, and yet become murderers. It is now history, but in the year 1099, July 14th, the Crusaders were successful in conquering Jeruslaem. Before they entered Jerusalem, they looked upon the great walls of this tremendous city, then they knelt down and thanked God. But what happened afterwards? Did they continue to thank God? Were these Crusaders filled with the Holy Spirit? Did they preach the liberating Gospel to the Jews and Arabs when they came to Jerusalem? None of it! They were instantly demonically possessed. An unbelievable thirst for blood came upon them. For eight days they did nothing else but murder the people of Jerusalem. History reports that they saw no difference in the Moslems or Jews, men or women, old people or children. All were murdered mercilessly. And the blood of men literally flowed in the streets of Jerusalem. The number of people murdered during that infamous Crusader week in Jerusalem is estimated to have been between 40,000 and even above 100,000 souls. That was one of the greatest victories of Satan because no one did more damage in the kingdom of God, in the proclamation of the Gospel, than these who carried the name "Christians." These Crusaders thought themselves to be armies of Christ. But in this place, here in Jerusalem, where the thrones of judgment are, they became the army of Satan, in spite of their very beautiful title "Crusaders." These bloodthirsty men who committed these atrocities and cold-blooded murders had embroidered on their coats large, beautiful crosses.

It is, therefore, not decisive *how* one goes to Jerusalem, but *what* one becomes when in Jerusalem. Here in Jerusalem, one is faced with a decision whether he wants to be not, and if he does not listen to the still, small voice of God, the leading of the Lord, he becomes instantly obedient to Satan and his demons. What Satan did with the Crusaders he is able to do today with Christians and even those who are missionaries but do not comply with the will of the Lord, who refuse to recognize the Almighty's intention for Israel and Jerusalem.

Our modern and enlightened time is marked with more bloodshed, violence and destruction than ever, since Noah's flood. Think about the horrible cruelties of today. Compare them with those of the Egyptians, the Assyrians, Medes, Persians, Greeks, Romans. It does not compare with any of them significantly because we are approaching the climax of cruelty. At the writing of these lines, it has not happened, but the third world war is standing at the door. Even now, while many would describe our time as a time of peace, there are literally hundreds of thousands of people who are dying daily either through local wars, terrorism, violence, or the cruel death of starvation because no one cares. Humanity is drowning, literally, in blood and tears. No one can deny that peace is taken away from earth today.

Who is to Blame for the Threat of War Today?

Generally speaking, it's always "them"; it's the "others"; it's the government and those certain leaders whom we hear so much about in the news media every day. What does the Bible say about it? *"Ye have heard that it was said by them of old time, Thou shalt not kill; and whosoever shall kill shall be in danger of the judgment: But I say unto you, That whosoever is angry with his brother without a cause shall be in danger of the judgment: and whosoever shall say to his brother, Raca, shall be in danger of the council: but whosoever shall say, Thou fool, shall be in danger of hell fire"* (Matthew 5:21,22). And in I John 3:15 we read, *"Whosoever hateth his brother is a murderer."* The climax of war is death. Where does it originate? It begins with hating your brother. Therefore, we can summarize: every individual living on the face of the earth is co-responsible for war and threat of war.

The beginning of war is not death but the end thereof is. The beginning is jealousy, anger and hate of the brother. To be angry against someone is the first step on the road of hate and murder. We must never underestimate our thoughts, because every thought has power, although invisible. Thoughts of man are of great importance, and mankind can be led to do evil or good through the power of thinking.

There was a flood of hate in Europe in 1914; it was

like a mighty river that threatened to flood its banks. Hate of one another was practiced and fostered to the point that it ended in the beginning of the first world war. It is very naive to believe that one certain gunshot started World War I; that war started in the hearts and minds of people long before that gunshot. We must see this very clearly. *We* have started war, not someone else. Not at a certain place or certain border but that war started and wars are starting today in the hearts of individuals! The thought of hate can spread quickly from your heart to the family, the church, to entire cities and even the country. War is the visible result of the invisible thoughts of evil toward one another.

At the end of this chapter may I ask you this question: Do you permit jealousy, quarrels, hate or anger in your heart? Then you are under the leadership of him who is the enemy of God. Therefore, come back to Him, the God who has created you. He has even paid for your evil thoughts with His own life on the cross of Calvary, in your place. It is as simple as that. Tell Jesus Christ, the Crucified and the Risen Saviour, all your sins and all your troubles. He is willing to forgive today and to heal you and to liberate you from them.

Chapter Three

God's Intended Action In The World Today

Things are happening today which never happened before in history. That is not a surprise because God never repeats Himself. Through the prophet Isaiah He called out thousands of years ago, *"Remember ye not the former things, neither consider the things of old. Behold, I will do a new thing; now it shall spring forth; shall ye not know it? I will even make a way in the wilderness, and rivers in the desert"* (Isaiah 43:18,19).

It is this holy "I will" which guarantees that His will, His plans, will be executed when the time has come to fulfill His prophecy. Not the will of man, but the holy will of God is being executed to its fullest extent even today. It is, furthermore, the fulfillment and ultimate answer to the prayer of our Lord Jesus, *"Thy will be done in earth, as it is in heaven"* (Matthew 6:10). All political movements we have seen in the past or see today cannot overcome the will of God but will serve for God's ultimate purpose, from the very least to the very greatest.

The Stars in the Sky

When God, the Lord, led Abraham out of his tent

during the night-time, He asked him to look up into the sky, *"And said, Look now toward heaven, and tell the stars, if thou be able to number them: and he said unto him, So shall thy seed be"* (Genesis 15:5). Abraham indeed had reason to doubt that promise, but he did not. According to historic writings, astronomers at that time had counted the stars and it is said that there were no more than 1,060 stars in the sky. Today, however, observing space with highly technological telescopes, it is estimated that the Milky Way alone consists of more than 100 billion suns, not counting the planets belonging to those suns. There is no scientist today who can tell how many such Milky Ways exist in the universe. In view of such unending largeness of the universe, man's numbering system becomes insignificant. We are talking much about space problems, but God has given so much room we could not imagine what to do with it. God can give to every human being one solar system for himself and there would still be an abundance left. From this point of view, how foolish, how insignificant and how little man really is with his so-much-praised space programs! For Abraham, however, and for us who believe, it is good to trust totally in God.

Not Explosion but Creation

While space is endless and incomprehensible for our limited and sin-darkened understanding, God also works in the smallest detail. Often scientists think they have discovered "it," but a little later someone discovers "it" again. Man indeed has made great progress in research and invention. To most of us the modern computer and other electronic machines are a scientific miracle. But in comparison with man's body, they are not even a little spoonful of water of the oceans of the world. Listening to scientific explanation about the cell of the human body and its function, one is simply amazed. On a small space, 1/10,000 of one millimeter, God has created precisely functioning chemical factories connected with power houses and internal transportation systems. Every function is exactly pre-programmed and works to a master plan unknown to our scientists. Today's computer world with its amazing achievement is able to process millions, even billions, of bits of information in a split second, yet it does not compare with the "computer" built into man. These tiny cells in the human body, invisible to the naked eye, contain more information than a 500 volume library (someone calculated). It can only be estimated, but the human body has more than 60 billion such cells. Such unthinkable, complicated precision is incomprehensible to man. All the universities of the world with their doctors and professors, throughout all the years of study, have discovered only a very insignificant part of the function of the human body. How very foolish the assumption is, as often heard today, "Everything came into being by itself. It was all an accident."

God's Intentions

Listen to what the Lord God says through the prophet Isaiah, *"Thus saith the LORD, the Holy One of Israel, and his Maker, Ask me of things to come concerning my sons, and concerning the work of my hands command ye me. I have made the earth, and created man upon it: I, even my hands, have stretched out the heavens, and all their host have I commanded"* (Isaiah 45:11,12). Through the Bible God speaks to us. We do well to heed what it says. He reveals to us His truth, *"The law of the Lord is perfect, converting the soul: the testimony of the Lord is sure, making wise the simple. The statutes of the Lord are right, rejoicing the heart: the commandment of the Lord is pure, enlightening the eyes. The fear of the Lord is clean, enduring for ever: the judgments of the Lord are true and righteous altogether. More to be desired are they than gold, yea, than much fine gold: sweeter also than honey and the honeycomb"* (Psalm 19:7-10). This very same Psalm also speaks about God's intention, about His judgments, His blessings through the sun, the moon, and the stars, *"The heavens declare the glory of God; and the firmament sheweth his handywork. Day unto day uttereth speech, and night unto night sheweth knowledge. There is no speech nor language, where their voice is not heard. Their line is gone out through all the earth, and their words to the end of the world. In them hath he set a tabernacle for the sun, Which is as a bridegroom coming out of his chamber, and rejoiceth as a strong*

The traditional prayer of Jews is being transformed into a prayer of expectation for the coming Messiah.

man to run a race. His going forth is from the end of the heaven, and his circuit unto the ends of it: and there is nothing hid from the heat thereof" (Psalm 19:1-6).

The Birth of a World Redeemer

The universe with its infinite space is connected to the Word of God. As a matter of fact, it is created by the Word of God, as is written in Hebrews 11:3, *"Through faith we understand that the worlds were framed by the word of God, so that things which are seen were not made of things which do appear."* God announced, for instance, the birth of the Lord Jesus Christ through a special star so that strangers who lived far away from the place of birth could recognize that the great King was born. How was it possible for these "Wise Men" of the east to recognize that this unusual star was there to announce the birth of the Messiah? They were Gentiles, astrologers, blind to the Word of God! Before we go into this matter, we must draw a line between astrology and astronomy.

Astrology equals a study which assumes and professes to interpret the influence of the heavenly bodies in human affairs. From the Bible's point of view, we reject astrology decidedly.

Astronomy equals the science of the heavenly bodies, their motions, positions, distance and magnitudes. We see that these two almost equal-sounding words are totally different, although both occupy themselves with the celestial bodies, the stars of the heavens. Astrology is based on assumption; astronomy is based on science.

From historic writings we know that astrology and astronomy were mixed up and counted as one and the same thing in the early days. Regarding the Babylonian astrology, B. Philberth writes in his book *Christliche Prophetie und Nuklearenergie* on pages 41 and 42 the following:

The birth of Jesus Christ, this mighty event in history, has been traced back by reliable astronomers to the great conjunction of Jupiter and Saturn. For the Babylonian astrologers it had a very special meaning. The threefold meeting of Jupiter and Saturn brought about the appearance of a special star which, seen from Babylonia, pointed toward the land of Israel. This very impressive discovery may have caused the king of Babylon to send his astrologers, or wise men, to Jerusalem to present special gifts unto the newborn king. Not only the report that a new king was born, but also this strange constellation of stars may have been the cause that *'Herod...was troubled, and all Jerusalem with him'* (Matthew 2:3).

Remarkable as it seems, this star pointed, during that hour, toward the small town of Bethlehem, the birthplace of Christ. That was the unique opportunity for the scribes in Jerusalem to identify Bethlehem as the birthplace of the Messiah according to the prophet Micah (Micah 5:2).

Not to be misunderstood: I have no intention to give credit to astrology in this matter. Independent of right or wrong, we must view historic astrology in its position at that time. No doubt, it was a significant power. In this rather surprising connection with astronomy and astrology using the constellations of the stars, God permitted, through this unique way, the birth of Jesus Christ to be announced to the heathens. From historic writings we know that these people could be compared with scientists of today, always searching for something, searching for the truth and indeed these wise men did find the truth. Thus we re-emphasize, astrology is a gimmick and often associated with the occult. But in early times, it was intermingled with science to a certain degree. Through it we also recognize that the living God permitted Himself to be recognized, even in the path of confusion, by seeking man.

Here we see that God can "hit straight with a crooked stick." These astrologers were obviously seeking the truth with all of their hearts and they found Him who is the Truth in person. That corresponds to the words of the Lord. He later said, *"Every one that is of the truth heareth my voice"* (John 18:37). From this we learn that the seeking of the truth with all of one's heart is decisive.

Regarding the star these Wise Men saw, William Wohrle writes the following:

During the year of the birth of Christ a unique threefold happening occurred in conjunction with Jupiter and Saturn in the asteric called Fish. Because for the Jews Saturn is the Sabbath star and Jupiter is the star of the King of righteousness, there was no doubt in the mind of the wise men from the East what the meaning of it was. This constellation had not occurred for 900 years and was expected with great excitement. It indicated the birth of the great King of the Jews. Furthermore, during this time there was a general desire among all the people of the world for a prince of peace, for a redeemer of the world who would be able to govern in righteousness. This expectation was even strengthened by the Babylonian astronomers, for they had the writings of the prophet Daniel who spoke about the coming of the Messiah. It was exactly on May 29th in the year 7 B.C., when these two stars, Jupiter and Saturn came closest. During the dawning of the day of April 12th they were approaching each other and became visible as one great bright star in the Middle Eastern sky. Obviously, these astronomers were very excited about it. Some of them may have remembered the prophecy of that strange heathen prophet Balaam who said that a Star would arise out of Jacob (Numbers 24:17). Should this be the time of fulfillment? Then on October 3rd, this strange assembly of stars occurred again (during that time these stars appeared much closer to each other than it was observed in 1940-1941 from many parts of the world). They had absolutely no more doubt that this constellation of the stars heralded the beginning of a new dispensation. This could only be the star of Moses of which the Jewish saga speaks. It claims that the star under which Moses, the great liberator of the people of Israel, was born would be the same star under which the Messiah would also be born, for Moses himself stated, *'The Lord thy God will raise up unto thee a Prophet from the midst of thee, of thy brethren, like unto me; unto him ye shall hearken'* (Deuteronomy 18:15). Finally on October 3rd, of 7 B.C., this star-conjunction appeared for the second time in a wonderful brightness in the heavens in the Middle East. That was the definite sign for the astronomers to arise and go to Palestine. They wanted to become witnesses of the beginning of a new dispensation. They must have been courageous and truth-seeking men and obviously very affluent to be able to get the necessary equipment and the customary gifts to honor this new King. They must have traveled a good six weeks. Jerusalem was their destination. There in the royal palace, the Saviour which had been announced by the king-star Jupiter must have been born. The direct procedure and how it all happened and ended is described for us in the four Gospels.

This shows us clearly that the universe is synchronized with the events God executes or plans to execute.

When we consider that the birth of Jesus Christ was the cause of a unique heavenly constellation, it is not surprising that when He, the Son of God, the greatest Son of Israel, was carrying away the sins of the entire world on the cross of Calvary, the entire universe was drawn into this world-shaking event. What did happen when Jesus was nailed to the cross? Another cosmic reaction took place! We read in Luke 23:44-46, *"And it was about the sixth hour, and there was a darkness over all the earth until the ninth hour. And the sun was darkened* [because Jesus the Sun of righteousness lost His life for us], *and the veil of the temple was rent in the midst. And when Jesus had cried with a loud voice, he said, Father, into thy hands I commend my spirit: and having said thus, he gave up the ghost."*

These signs in the heavens were not limited to the outer space but occurred in conjunction with the action on earth. Much has been written and much has been speculated regarding heavenly signs during the re-unification of the city of Jerusalem in 1967. There are many facts which speak for themselves. But we can be assured that a prophetic act did take place. Statistically it can be proven that with 1967, with the liberation of Jerusalem, the quality and moral character of the Gentile nations has been decreasing rapidly ever since. This coincides precisely with the prophecy of the Lord when He says, *"and Jerusalem shall be trodden down of the Gentiles, UNTIL the times of the Gentiles be fulfilled"* (Luke 21:24). The beginning of Jewish rule of Jerusalem is the beginning of the end of the Gentile nations!

We repeat, timewise, the fulfillment of prophetic events may be separated by many years, yet they do belong together. Listen how God showed the patriarch Abraham a prophetic vision using the stars of heaven, *"By myself have I sworn, saith the Lord, for because thou hast done this thing, and hast not withheld thy son, thine only son: That in blessing I will bless thee, and in multiplying I will multiply thy seed as the stars of the heaven, and as the sand which is upon the sea shore"* (Genesis 22:16,17). That wasn't fulfilled right away. Even hundreds of years later, Moses reminded the Lord of that very same promise, *"Remember Abraham, Isaac, and Israel, thy servants, to whom thou swarest by thine own self, and saidst unto them, I will multiply your seed as the stars of heaven, and all this land that I have spoken of will I give unto your seed, and they shall inherit it for ever"* (Exodus 32:13).

From this we see that God is not bound timewise, but He does fulfill His Word IN time. To summarize, the sign from heaven that was seen in the form of a star heralding the coming of the world Saviour synchronized the movements of heaven with the event occurring on earth!

Satan's Prophecy

God is the originator of all things, and from Scripture we know that Satan is the great imitator. God spoke through the mouths of the prophets about the coming of the Saviour and He caused signs to be seen. We can rightly ask, "What signs are there for the coming of the Antichrist?" The answer is one word—apostasy! A further question seems natural to ask, "Is the Antichrist already among us?" Indeed, we can assume he is. Because we are standing so close to the time of the Second Coming of Christ, the devil is forced to reveal his intention, too. Let us see an example at Christ's first coming. When He was on earth, the demonic powers on earth had to reveal themselves. They even had to tell the truth, *"What have we to do with thee, Jesus, thou Son of God, art Thou come hither to torment us before the time?"* (Matthew 8:29). Later, even in the presence of the Apostles, Satan was forced to expose himself, and again he had to tell the truth, *"These men are the servants of the most high God, which shew unto us the way of salvation"* (Acts 16:17). Satan has his messengers, too. Although they tell a lot of deceptive lies, they mingle it with some truth. Back in 1963, November 22nd, Jean Dixon, a soothsayer (demonically-inspired), stated to her friend, "I am very, very nervous today. Something terrible will happen to our President." A little later, the news media around the world proclaimed that President Kennedy was assassinated. This same woman published another vision she had, "February 3, 1962, at 7:00 a.m. a child was born in the Middle East of a poor peasant family who will change the order of the world." Soothsayers and fortune tellers usually agree that their predictions are about 50% accurate. We compare the Bible with this and come to a totally different configuration regarding accuracy:

> Some 845 prophetic statements by more than one dozen different prophets about the birth, the life and the dying of the Son of God, Jesus Christ, can be found in the Bible. Every single statement was

literally fulfilled, although some were made more than a thousand years before the birth of Jesus. The prophet Daniel, for instance, gives us eight statements about the life of Jesus. Using mathematic configuration in attempting to find the accuracy of the fulfillment of these predictions, we would be faced with the astronomical number of 1 to 100,000,000,000 possibilities. Such mathematical results eliminate coincidence. Thus we see that only God, in His omnipotent position, could cause these possibilities of fulfillment to come about in the right time, the right place, in the right succession and therewith confirming the reliability of Bible prophecy.

I again point out that the devil and his heralds often speak deceptive lies but it can also be a self-exposing of the enemy in view of the soon-coming of our Lord Jesus. In any case, this day of the birth of the Antichrist will be a cursed day, a day which will bring the greatest catastrophe upon the world. Job, when he spoke about his own day of birth, prophetically viewed that horrible day, too, because Satan was permitted by God to play havoc with him, *"Let the day perish wherein I was born, and the night in which it was said, There is a man child conceived. Let that day be darkness; let not God regard it from above, neither let the light shine upon it. Let darkness and the shadow of death stain it; let a cloud dwell upon it; let the blackness of the day terrify it. As for that night, let darkness seize upon it; let it not be joined unto the days of the year, let it not come into the number of the months. Lo, let that night be solitary, let no joyful voice come therein. Let them curse it that curse the day, who are ready to raise up their mourning. Let the stars of the twilight thereof be dark; let it look for light, but have none; neither let it see the dawning of the day: Because it shut not up the doors of my mother's womb, nor hid sorrow from mine eyes"* (Job 3:3-10).

We do not attempt to prove that the Antichrist was born February 3, 1962, but we will keep three facts in mind that indicate the coming of Christ is at hand, and consequently the Antichrist must be born before He returns:

1. The Antichrist is on his way because his spirit is working mightily.
2. We are approaching the end of the sixth millennium since the creation of man.
3. The kingdom of the Antichrist, that is the Roman World Empire, is receiving increasingly visible forms.

The Borders of the Roman World Empire

The extent of the Roman Empire as it existed some 2,000 years ago will have to be re-established. For what purpose? Because the first and the second coming of Jesus are as one from a prophetic point of view. The Bible says, *"One day is with the Lord as a thousand years, and a thousand years as one day"* (II

Peter 3:8). The Roman Empire is being re-shaped geographically into its original forms today. For example, Northern Europe never belonged to the Roman Empire, thus lately, we hear much about the displeasure of the Scandinavian countries with NATO. Leading in this opposition is Norway which never was affected by the old Roman Empire. Press reports we read today contain fulfillment of Bible prophecy. Not long ago, an interesting article appeared in the publication *Europa*.

(Norway)

Stanislaw Shtshebotov, first Secretary of the Soviet Embassy in Norway, has participated extensively in underground activity in that country. He is constantly on the move to persuade members of parliament and politicians to oppose the course of the Western oriented Norwegian government and instead support Soviet foreign policy. This so-called diplomat is not an unknown person. Several years ago, while working as an officer of the KGB, he was caught in espionage activity in Denmark and subsequently expelled from the country.

(Denmark)

In political circles in Denmark, worries are being expressed about Oleg Espersen, who was appointed Minister of Justice during the last formation of the new government. Defense documents bring charges against Espersen showing extensive connection with

East European and Soviet diplomats. Many Danes have considered him a security risk ever since. One fact is proved: Espersen is one of the members of government who has expressed his so-called neutral stand and therewith revealed himself as a strong opponent to NATO.

Anti-NATO propaganda is sweeping Denmark lately. Soviet political experts are permitted to teach rather extensively in schools in Copenhagen. The main subjects of these lectures are in opposition to Western ideology. They are showing the danger of NATO plans for Denmark and the surrounding countries. The infiltration of pro-Soviet ideology is increasing rapidly.

(Sweden)

Just recently, the Swedish foreign minister, Ullsten, revealed in his debate a one-sided, anti-American policy regarding El Salvador, while failing to mention Moscow's foreign policy and especially the invasion of Afghanistan.

(Finland)

Finland, for one, has no intention whatsoever to be united with the ECC because it has never belonged to the Roman Empire and, therefore, is very friendly to Moscow.

(Germany)

Take Germany. It is not a coincidence that Germany was divided into two countries with barbed wire

Poland lives under military oppression. The peace it desires is taken away.... Added to that the abundance of consumer goods are gone; shelves are mostly empty.

through the heart of it, watchtowers erected along its border and many deadly and highly sophisticated mine-fields along the center of Germany. The reason? East Germany never belonged to the Roman World Empire! Even today, the northern part of West Germany is in great danger of being invaded by Soviet forces. Why? Again, that part has never belonged to the original Roman Empire. Even the political system in West Germany today is strongly divided. There are political parties who reject outright any closer relationship with the Soviet Union. Others welcome and even fight vehemently for union with the Soviets. Thus we see that the united Europe which will come to be, will correspond to the original borders of the Roman World Empire as it was during Christ's time.

The East

(East-Germany)

Eastern Europe and Asia are under the authority of world communism. It has been established through force and shedding of blood. Remember what happened to East Germany in the fifties or to Hungary in 1956? The attempt for freedom, the attempt to shake off the yoke of communism was crushed unmercifully. The *J.C.G. Publication* writes:

(Hungary)

The tragedies occurring in this land cannot be fully

understood if one is not familiar with the history of
Hungarian Jews during the thirties. The decimation
of the Jewish population was not only the result of
Germany's occupation of that country in 1944, but
was also the result of Hungary's treatment of its own
Jews. Especially in the Hungarian annexed area,
strong anti-Jewish laws were instituted whose
brutality can only be compared with Nazi-Germany's.
The establishment of ghettos, concentration camps
and deportations by the Nazi forces only concluded
the work the Hungarians had started themselves.

(Czechoslovakia)

Later, the attempt of the Czechoslovakian people
was also suffocated in blood by world communism.
Not long ago, we saw the swift action in Poland. All
these tragedies are nothing other than God-permitted
judgments upon these countries. We only need to read
recent history and we will understand what is written
in Deuteronomy 32:8, *"When the Most High divided to
the nations their inheritance, when he separated the
sons of Adam, he set the bounds of the people according
to the number of the children of Israel."*

(Poland)

The horrible events happening in Poland today are
not a coincidence. History, barely one generation old,
proves that in Poland the Jewish people suffered
more than anywhere else. Poland has always been
strongly anti-Semitic. Pogroms were the order of the

day throughout the centuries. This type of anti-Semitism was brutally expressed during the Nazi regime. Following is a quote from the *Jüdische Enzyklopadie:*

> The Polish population was always vehemently anti-German, but the majority of them were also violently anti-Semitic. Many Poles were convinced that the Jewish casualties were not better than the murderers themselves. Jews who had luckily escaped from a ghetto were often caught and murdered by Poles themselves. Poles too willingly helped the Nazis to uncover hiding places of the Jews, and it was not a rare occasion when they helped kill them. Especially the Polish police, with only a few exceptions, played a tragic role in this matter. Of all the Nazi-invaded countries, Poland was the place where most Jews were murdered.
>
> During the German invasion in September, 1939, there were 3,351,000 Jews living in Poland. At the end of the Nazi regime, over 3,000,000 had been murdered. Even in 1945, at the end of the war, in the city of Chrakau, an additional 400 surviving Jews were murdered.

Poland has heaped upon itself a great burden of guilt and today she is experiencing the shocking truth of the Word of God, *"I will bless them that bless thee, and curse him that curseth thee"* (Genesis 12:3). In spite of the horrible judgment Poland is experiencing, anti-Semitism has again flamed in this country where there are barely any Jews. Dan Kurzmann writes in his book *The Bravest Battle* the following:

> Horrible anti-Semitic campaigns were discovered by Western diplomats during the military regime campaign in Warsaw against its opponent, Solidarity. In a country with an insignificant number of Jewish citizens, anti-Semitism is still a favored propaganda tool. Offices of the formerly free union, Solidarity, were painted with Stars of David. Even propaganda leaflets printed by the military regime against Solidarity were marked with the Star of David. The state-controlled radio in Warsaw openly blamed the crisis on the activity of the chauvinistic Jewish International. Even the *Trybuna Ludu*, the official publication of the Communist party in Poland, used anti-Zionist propaganda in its attack on the union. The publication outrageously accused Jewish Solidarity and human rights activist, history professor Bronislav Geremek, one of the closest advisors to Lech Walesas, of treason. He was accused with other Jews, Adam Michnik and Jaczek Kuron, to have organized Zionistic demonstrations during the Six-Day war.

Whenever force and brutality are used, it is against God, and therewith it pinpoints itself first against the Jews. World communism, which represents the anti-God movement, is established through force and bloodshed and will end in bloodshed, to be precise, on the mountains and in the valleys of Israel. Here we also must point out the unwilling cooperation of Russia's satellites who are forced into line by her power. But when the time and opportunity will come, they will turn against one another exactly as it is written, *"Every man's sword shall be against his brother"* (Ezekiel 38:21).

Although we see sufficient evidence of the signs in the heavens and the signs on earth which point to the near end of the world, we do not know exactly when the year of judgment will be. Maybe it is this year that the threatening third world war will explode into reality. But on the basis of the Scripture, we know that the Rapture, the sudden taking away of all true believers in the Lord Jesus, is very close. And it will happen during the restoration of Israel which is now in full progress. The re-establishment of Israel started in 1948. That should tell anyone how late it really is!

God's Covenant People, Israel

The Jewish people are being brought back to the land of their fathers because it is God's will and purpose. The more Jews come back to the land of Israel the stronger the nation will be. But at the same time, it causes the weakening of the nations of the world. Why? Because the climax of it will be judgment upon all nations in the measure they have dealt with the Jews. At the writing of this book, Israel has signed only one peace treaty with one Arab country, Egypt. Is there real peace between the two countries? No! Israel is being deceived by Egypt continuously, while the world looks upon Egypt as a peace-loving and conservative country. The *Near East Report* of December 24, 1982, tells us the following:

> Mohammed Heikal, former editor of the Cairo daily *Al-Ahram* and a Nasser confidante, says that the Egyptian people reject normalization with Israel. He told the Beirut weekly *Monday Morning* that the Israeli ambassador in Cairo was among the first to feel the frost. 'Initially the first Israeli ambassador to Egypt was invited to various embassies which also invited Egyptians. Soon, any Egyptian invited by an embassy—even an Egyptian from the bourgeoisie, who are receptive to ideas of peace and openness— began asking if the Israeli ambassador would be among the guests, and if the answer was yes, that Egyptian would not accept the invitation. Eventually, the Israeli ambassador found himself dealing with a very limited circle.... He was dying of boredom and he left. A second ambassador was sent...but the Egyptian people put him in a 'deep freeze.' Heikal says that the anti-Israel sentiment in Egypt 'was there before the Lebanon developments.'

The January 4, 1983, issue of *Newsview* adds another event:

> Egyptian Ambassador to Israel Sa'ad Mortada, currently on recall to Cairo until an Israeli withdrawal from Lebanon hopefully thaws the now-frozen normalization process, has been spending much of his time lecturing his countrymen on the whys and wherefores of Israel. After several such talks, Mortada concluded that the degree of ignorance

among his countrymen of what goes on just north of their border is scandalous. 'On the other hand, Israelis are very well informed on events in Egypt, though their perceptions are not always accurate,' he said. Mortada also availed himself of the free time afforded by the lull in formal relations to pay a courtesy call on his fellow 'countryman.' Egyptian-born Israeli Ambassador to Egypt Moshe Sasson, unlike his visitor, is still very hard at work trying to make a go of relations despite recent setbacks.

After the return of the last part of Sinai to Egypt in April, 1982, Israel was disappointedly awakened. Suddenly, they realized that part of the Promised Land was surrendered to a nation which has never owned the Sinai legally. One day in the future, Israel will have to shed the blood of its young soldiers again in order to repossess that part of the Promised Land. The Word of God has warned about the reliance on Egypt very clearly. *"Now, behold, thou trustest upon the staff of this bruised reed, even upon Egypt, on which if a man lean, it will go into his hand, and pierce it: so is Pharaoh king of Egypt unto all that trust on him"* (II Kings 18:21).

Israel's Victories

Today, the danger for the little country of Israel is growing overwhelmingly. But Psalm 121:4 says, *"Behold, he that keepeth Israel shall neither slumber nor sleep."* From a visible point of view, Israel has no

real chance of survival but invisibly they have the
protection of God the Creator, and the nations who
have gone against Israel in the past have noticed it
each time they come in battle contact. When Israel
liberated Lebanon from the PLO, in June 1982, the
Syrian soldiers experienced something of the invisible
God. The absolute victory of Israel's armed forces was
illogical. Even until this day, military experts in the
world are discussing it, attempting to find some
sensible explanation. Not only were the Arab states
shamefully defeated but with it their Russian allies
and supporters received the unexpected shock. Their
most sophisticated and highly praised war machinery
was totally helpless against Israel's action. American
news media quickly praised the American-manufac-
tured weapons highly, but strangely enough, these
same weapons failed miserably against the Russian
weapons in Viet Nam! The world press was reluctant
to give Israel credit for its bravery and expertise.
Therewith the world is not only rejecting Israel but is
rejecting the living God who is helping Israel. In spite
of all, danger for Israel is increasing tremendously,
but the end of danger will come soon when the
Messiah will come for His people and liberate them
totally.

The Prophetic Word for You

Let us now put the spotlight of the Prophetic Word
on our personal lives. With open eyes we are seeing the

signs of the times, and we recognize how very precise the Word of God is. Therefore, we do well to take heed to the words, *"But the end of all things is at hand: be ye therefore sober, and watch unto prayer"* (I Peter 4:7). This "end of all things" includes everything, the world, time and humanity. Man is the most penetrating and obvious sign of the end-times. Just think about the terrorists which are active today around the world, and no limit is set for them any longer. The Apostle Paul wrote to his co-worker some 1,900 years ago, *"This know also, that in the last days perilous times shall come. For men shall be lovers of their own selves, covetous, boasters, proud, blasphemers, disobedient to parents, unthankful, unholy, Without natural affection, trucebreakers, false accusers, incontinent, fierce, despisers of those that are good, Traitors, heady, high-minded, lovers of pleasures more than lovers of God"* (II Timothy 3:1-4). Does this Scripture identify our time? Indeed, it does.

In this time in which we live, while we realize and sense that everything is ready to collapse, we must realize that God is confronting us with His holy will. God is promising to you very personally, *"Behold, I will do a new thing; now it shall spring forth; shall ye not know it? I will even make a way in the wilderness, and rivers in the desert"* (Isaiah 43:19). If your heart has become a wilderness and a desert, then God is willing even today to create something new, even during this last hour.

An Invitation

Friend, you have sensed it when reading this book that those things we have written are the truth because they come from the Bible and the Bible is the Word of God. Do you have the assurance in your heart that you will escape the horrible things which are about to happen? Escape not to another place but into utter, endless, eternal glory? Do you have peace with God because Jesus Christ lives in your heart through faith? If your answer is negative, permit me to ask another question. Do you yearn for peace? Now you may have questions such as, How can I change it all? How can I obtain peace with God? How can I receive the forgiveness of sins which I have committed in thoughts, words and deeds? How can I know I will go to heaven? Is there such a thing at all in this hectic time that there is someone who does care for me to whom I can tell the deepest needs of my heart? Someone who is faithful and will not disappoint me, who gives sense and direction to my life and fills me with peace and joy?

To all of these questions, God Himself is willing to give an answer in a wonderful way. Therefore continue to read attentively the last chapter.

Chapter Four
Peace With God

The peace with God, which man has lost, is the highest and most exalted peace there is. Shortly after sin entered men, peace was taken from the earth. War broke out in Adam and Eve's family. Cain murdered his brother, Abel. Since then, there has been no more peace. History is marked by bloodshed and tears. Yet to this day, we hear men saying, "Peace, peace! No more war!" But there has never been abiding peace because war and strife are in the heart of every single human being.

Every person in all of history, no matter how important, was wrong when he stated, "We have made peace." Even the politicians of today are dead wrong when they claim, "We are working for peace." We can summarize with one sentence the situation of mankind, "There is no peace." Thus we must investigate the origin of war and at the same time ask the question, "Can there be peace?"

We've seen in detail in chapter 2 the origin of war. Now let us apply this fact very personally to ourselves.

James describes the position so aptly in James 4:1, *"From whence come wars and fightings among you? come they not hence, even of your lusts that war in your members?"* War is in the hearts of men thus the war-threat will not be removed by demonstrations. The danger of war can only be dealt with on a spiritual level and not on a political or ideological level. What did Jesus say in Matthew 15:19? *"For out of the heart proceed evil thoughts, murders, adulteries, fornications, thefts, false witness, blasphemies."* Did you notice the first thing that comes from the evil thoughts of our hearts? MURDER! After murder follow the rest... adulteries, fornications, thefts, etc. The first thing that comes from our heart is therefore war. War is the desire to do away with an opponent. Wickedness, wrath, strife, and discord follow.

Is Peace Possible?

The origin of war is in the heart of man. This being the case, as we have just seen from the Bible, we must ask the questions, "Can that be changed? Can our hearts produce thoughts of peace instead of war?" The answer is definitely Yes. We indeed CAN have peace in our hearts if we have peace with God. God, the Creator of man, Himself paved the way from His heart to yours and mine through His Son, Jesus Christ. That was the meaning of the angel's message to the shepherds, *"Peace, good will toward men"* (Luke 2:14). God wants to restore the peace between Him and man.

When we read history, even recent history, we sense a longing for peace amidst all the troubles and unrest, especially in Israel. In the Bible, too, we see this yearning for peace, e.g. Isaiah 26:12, *"Lord, thou wilt ordain peace for us."* Isaiah 27:5, *"Or let him take hold of my strength, that he may make peace with me; and he shall make peace with me."* Those who lived under the Old Covenant did not have peace available to them as we have today. The same prophet, Isaiah, also wrote in chapter 48:22, *"There is no peace, saith the Lord, unto the wicked."* Sin divides us from peace. These sorts of people are driven from one place to the next, harassed and worried, under a continual, yet undue stress, all because they have no peace in their hearts. Therefore, Isaiah also foresaw with prophetic clarity the One who would bring us this missing peace through His substitutionary suffering and death on the cross of Calvary. *"The chastisement of OUR PEACE was upon him; and with his stripes we are healed"* (Isaiah 53:5).

I can tell you most assuredly that if sin robs you of peace, the punishment or chastisement of your sin lay on Him so that you can have peace. Many people know this theoretically and even agree with it, but they still have no peace, despite Calvary. Why is this? Are you one who believes that Jesus died to take away your sins so that you have peace, but in actual fact you do not have the peace of God in your heart? Do you need to be in a good mood to feel peace in your heart? Or do you need a mountain-top experience? What a miserable position to be in! Why is it that so many believers do not experience the peace of God in actual fact? Isaiah 48:18 gives us the answer, *"O that thou hadst hearkened to my commandments! then had thy peace been as a river, and thy righteousness as the waves of the sea."* This shows that when the Lord requires faith of us it also includes obedience. In fact, true faith is obedience. Faith means to do what He says in His Word. Faith is not a passive thing but rather active and dynamic. That is why it says of our Lord Jesus Christ who brought us peace, *"Though he were a Son, yet learned he obedience by the things which he suffered; And being made perfect, he became the author of eternal salvation unto all them that OBEY him"* (Hebrews 5:8,9).

Jesus Has Established Peace With God for Us

It is a wonderful experience to have the peace of God in one's heart in a world of strife and trouble. Romans 5:1 says, *"Therefore being justified by faith, we have PEACE with God through our Lord Jesus Christ."* Otherwise, peace with God is impossible. He is holy, and we are sinners and fall short of the glory of God. Although God and sinners are mutually exclusive, THROUGH JESUS CHRIST we have been reconciled: we now have peace with God. So the question is: Do you have Jesus? Do you have this peace? *"He is our peace,"* says Ephesians 2:14. Colossians 2:14 tells HOW He made this peace for us, *"Blotting out the handwriting of ordinances that was against us, which was contrary to us, and took it out of the way, nailing it to his cross."* It was necessary for Jesus to die such a death in order for us to have peace.

Romans 5:1 also tells us what we have to do in order to have this peace, *"Therefore being justified by FAITH, we have peace with God."* Faith is a wonderful mystery, and yet the word "faith," has become so commonplace that it is no longer understood. From God's point of view, everything necessary for men to have peace has been done through Jesus Christ. But you must believe. That is the triumph of faith; that is true peace with God!

Not everyone, however, comes to a true, genuine faith in the Lord Jesus Christ. Paul already wrote to the Christians in Thessalonica saying, *"All men have not faith"* (II Thessalonians 3:2). Why not? It is because so many people let themselves be easily influenced by the "confuser," that is, Satan. He is the one who deceives us. He causes us to mistake feelings for faith. He separates faith from the Person of Jesus Christ. People often say, "Oh, I believe in God!" and yet they do not know Jesus personally. That is an example of dividing faith from the Word. Faith and the Word of God are one, while feelings are another matter. Whoever dares to go against his feelings and put his faith in Jesus will not be put to shame.

Only the faith in a personal Saviour, in the Lord Jesus Christ, results in true peace with God, because this faith activates the precious blood which He has shed on the cross for you. That type of faith comes from your heart, *"For with the heart man believeth unto righteousness"* (Romans 10:10). Therefore, it is absolutely essential that you rely *not* on your feelings, but on that which is written, *"For the Scripture saith, Whosoever believeth on Him shall not be ashamed"* (Romans 10:11).

The Greatest Victory of All Time

The word "triumph" is used twice in the New Testament. It is used to describe the victory of Jesus and our victory in Him when He made peace with God for us through His own blood. He triumphed over all the powers of the enemy on the cross of Calvary, *"Having spoiled principalities and powers, he made a shew of them openly, triumphing over them in it"* (Colossians 2:15). On the cross Jesus has openly triumphed over all those things which are the cause of your troubles and distress. This victory is eternally valid and is indisputable. Satan and his demons are defeated by Jesus Christ once and for all!

Jesus is Victor! Therefore, it is foolish when we let ourselves be affected by the devil, by powers of depression, suffering or unbelief, because Jesus has deprived all dark powers of their authority and strength in an open triumph.   He is the Author and FINISHER of our faith. All who say "Yes" to Jesus also enter into His triumph. They can triumph even in a peaceless world. The peace of God which passes all understanding rules in their hearts (Philippians 4:7).

Peace marches are popular but peace in the heart is lacking.
The Nero Cross is often visible.

In II Corinthians 2:14 we read, *"Now thanks be unto God, which always causeth us to triumph in Christ, and maketh manifest the savour of his knowledge by us in every place."* This may sound strange in the ears of those not born-again, but it is true. It is a wonderful truth, that those who are born-again of the Spirit of God have this peace of God in their hearts. As a matter of fact we who believe even manifest, that is, we radiate, this wonderful peace into the world. We actually give this peace of God to a world which lies in unrest, turmoil, violence and war. Hence, believers are admonished in the Word of God, *"Follow peace with all men, and holiness, without which no man shall see the Lord"* (Hebrews 12:14). This tells us that all who have the peace of God in their hearts should do everything to have this peace transferred to others. Now the question comes to mind, what if others purposely do me wrong and I am displeased with them? Answer: the peace of God will overcome this, too, and the peace will remain in my heart and I will be able to love these people, too, to bless them and to pray for them without having any thoughts of revenge in my heart against them. I have peace with God and, therefore, peace with my brothers and sisters. This is the triumph of faith in Christ. This is peace with God!

Deceptive Peace

For what sort of peace is the world today seeking with their demonstrations and protest marches? We see all sorts of slogans on banners. Often the Nero cross, the inverted cross, is used in these peace demonstrations. It is a deceptive peace! Although they are shouting for peace, war is raging in the heart of every one. Here is a short summary of the history of today's popular "peace sign." Erich Sauer describes the "peace sign" in his book, *Offenbarung Gottes und Antword des Glaubens:*

During the Middle Ages, the peace sign, as it is called today, was used and named for different purposes. It was called the witch's foot, the Nero's cross, and often the Cobalt-foot. This sign is in popular use until this day in the occult. Bertram Russell is the one responsible for the re-creation of this sign. Russell was a determined atheist. In one of his writings, he expressed himself with these words, 'I sincerely hope that every form of religious faith will die.' This peace sign was propagated by him for the first time in 1958. It was during the Easter peace march in England. The purpose of this protest march was aimed against nuclear weapons. It also propagated a one-sided disarmament of Great Britain. Thousands of students marched in protest requesting NATO to unite with the Communists. Bertram Russell claimed to have designed this symbol for these demonstrations. He called it the peace sign. Atheist Russell believed that the ultimate victory of world Communism would be desirable, thus his slogan, 'Better red than dead.' His claim is, however, not correct, for he is not the creator of this 'peace sign'; he merely re-popularized it. This sign can be found throughout history as a sign of expression of hate against God. It can be seen everywhere in the world today; mostly young people but older people also wear it. Without doubt, this is one of the preview signs of the Antichrist. While this sign is being exhibited during demonstrations against war by the so-called peace groups, it is rather striking that this sign is not seen during demonstrations against Communism. Summarizing, this false peace sign was used during the Middle Ages as a symbol for black magic and is a sign of blasphemy against the living God.

Every and all peace movements in the world will not achieve a genuine peace. In actual fact, it is the invisible rebellion against the peace of God. This rebellion within the heart of man against God's peace results in war. May it be the Cold War, or even the threatening arms race mushrooming today, it is the result of the lack of peace with God.

What sort of peace were the philosophers speaking about and seeking after? They were all looking for the same, for peace, but without faith. The celebrated German poet, Goethe, gave his recipe for peace as follows: "Cultivate a worthy hobby which satisfies you in good days and uplifts you in bad days. Read daily in the Bible or in Homer, or contemplate beautiful paintings, or listen to good music. Search for something that satisfies you in every situation and under all circumstances to achieve that comfortable feeling."

But this highly gifted man apparently did not find peace with God for he himself wrote, "When I die, write on my grave stone, 'During life he had many happy experiences but real happiness he never found.'" This world-renowned man, Goethe, was one of the most unhappy ones. He did not achieve peace with God through faith in Jesus Christ. His last words were, "Mehr Licht!" (More light!). In spite of his intellectual greatness, he was in darkness because he did not have the peace of God within his heart.

This is the situation of many intelligent people today, perhaps even among my readers right now. Do YOU have peace with God? This is the great topic of the Bible. In the beginning of almost all of Paul's letters he writes, *"Grace to you and PEACE FROM GOD our Father and our Lord Jesus Christ"* (Romans 1:7; I Corinthians 1:3; II Corinthians 1:2; Galatians 1:3, etc.).

Business With Fear

We are facing, in a unique way, a catastrophic world war, which is the reason for the politicians' feverish traveling from one place to the next, from one to another peace conference; yet the world situation continues to deteriorate.

Fear has grasped humanity, and we are reminded of what Jesus said in Luke 21:26, *"Men's hearts failing them for fear, and for looking after those things which are coming on the earth: for the powers of heaven shall be shaken."* The greatest sickness today is fear. Most people are psychologically sick because of fear. That is the result of not having peace with God.

There is fear of war, fear of a Russian invasion, fear of a nuclear catastrophe, fear of cancer, fear of a heart attack, fear in business, fear of almost anything you can name. People are even using this fact as a means of generating profitable business. The following appeared recently in a German newspaper:

> It is five minutes to twelve. Make provision for the ultimate day... War, crises and conflicts are increasing in the old world. You must make provision for the future...find a safe place of refuge. By the time gold is being exchanged for bread, and valuable diamonds for a plane ticket, countries who are safe will have set up barriers preventing Europeans from emigrating, and the lights in Europe will most certainly have gone out. But we have made provision for you; there are islands in the Caribbean reserved for you. We invite a limited number of like-minded people to take part in our enterprise! Write to...

What a deception! As if one is safe on an island! There is no peace of God in the Caribbean, either. But there really is only one place of safety, "Safe in the arms of Jesus." Peace with God through our Lord Jesus Christ is the only place of absolute safety and security. It is with the Person, the Crucified, Resurrected and soon-returning Lord. That is the only genuine peace, that is, peace of the heart, which is so real and so wonderful that the Bible says it passes all understanding. If you are fearful of today or of the future, then your fear is legitimate, because Jesus said in Luke 21:26, *"For the powers of heaven shall be shaken."* This is what men fear. They sense that there is something in the air. Some talk of a world catastrophe; others say a breakdown of the universe; others fear a collision of the planets. Even reliable and respectable scientists today predict a possible cosmic catastrophe. There is much mathematical calculation going on about the re-appearing of Halley's comet in 1986. This time it could collide with the earth, it is said.

Do you know the deepest reason for man's fear, even though he cannot define it? It is the shaking of the powers of heaven, because when the Son of Man appears in power and great glory, then the powers of heaven will be shaken. The Bible speaks about this time and identifies it as the return of Jesus Christ. All men who live in rebellion against God do not have the peace of God in their hearts and for that they are trembling, whether they realize it or not. But believers, the children of God, rejoice because they have already experienced these powers of heaven.

The Resurrection Power of Jesus Christ

Although the powers of heaven are hidden from the physical eye, they have been confirmed by millions upon millions of those who believe in the power of Jesus Christ. For believers it has been an indisputable reality for almost 2,000 years, that is, the dying and resurrection of Jesus Christ. This unlimited power of

"Cain rose up against Abel his brother, and slew him" (Genesis 4:8).

As a result, man is filled with fear. During a Protestant church day demonstration in West Germany, a banner rightly proclaimed *furchtet euch* (be ye fearful)!

God is described for us in Ephesians 1:19-22, *"And what is the exceeding greatness of his power to us-ward who believe, according to the working of his mighty power, Which he wrought in Christ, when he raised him from the dead, and set him at his own right hand in the heavenly places, far above all principality, and power, and might, and dominion, and every name that is named, not only in this world, but also in that which is to come: And hath put all things under his feet, and gave him to be the head over all things to the church."* These powers were set free through the Lord Jesus Christ when God raised him from the dead, *"...the exceeding greatness of his power...which he wrought in Christ, when he raised him from the dead, and set him at his own right hand in the heavenly places."* That is another reason why we have peace with God. These powers are a hidden reality in our lives. The powers of heaven broke through to this earth with the resurrection of our Lord.

The Creating Power of Faith

Now we come to the question, "What is and what will be the result of these heavenly powers?" It results in absolute peace for all who believe and in destruction for the world which rebels against it. "And this is the exceeding greatness of his power TO US-WARD WHO BE-LIEVE." Through believing in Jesus we have peace with God.

Again, I must emphasize so that I will not be

misunderstood. Faith itself does not save and does not transfer the power of heaven to us, but what counts is the content of faith, and this content must be Jesus Christ and Him alone. The person, Jesus Christ, is *"Christ the power of God, and the wisdom of God"* (I Corinthians 1:24).

Dear friend, do you have no power in your faith? Are you, in actual fact, lonely and do not have the peace of God in your heart? The reason for that is that your faith, until this very day, is not centered on the Person, Jesus Christ!

Look at the heroes of faith in your Bible. Their faith was related to and not separate from the Lord Himself. In Hebrews 11:11, we read of Sara, who at the age of ninety, through faith, *"received strength to conceive seed, and was delivered of a child when she was past age, because SHE JUDGED HIM FAITHFUL WHO HAD PROMISED."* She received strength, not through faith in something, but through faith in a Person. She did not consider the fact that she was ninety, for she had peace with God. She believed that what God had promised He could also fulfill. This is a good example for you, too.

This power that leads to peace with God is called "exceeding great" (Ephesians 1:19). If Jesus Christ in person is divine power and divine peace and He upholds all things by the word of His power, *"Who being the brightness of his glory, and the express image of his person, and upholding all things by the word of his power, when he had by himself purged our sins, sat down on the right hand of the Majesty on high"* (Hebrews 1:3), how great must be His strength to bear! He upholds *all things*; that includes YOU.

Power to Bear

He upholds all things BY THE WORD OF HIS POWER! Do you see from this the immeasurable power of the Word of God?! That is why Jesus said, *"The words that I speak unto you, they are spirit, and they are life"* (John 6:63). Do you remember what Isaiah 9:6 says? *"The government shall be upon his shoulder."* That shows that He is so mighty that He only needs one shoulder to carry the whole universe! Yet, as the good Shepherd when finding the lost sheep, the Scripture says, *"And when he hath found it, he layeth it on his shoulders, rejoicing"* (Luke 15:5). Now He uses both shoulders! He uses His whole strength for you. *"And even to your old age I am he; and even to hoar hairs will I carry you: I have made, and I will bear; even I will carry, and will deliver you"* (Isaiah 46:4). He carries you together with your burdens. That is why it is possible to have peace with God. It is often the circumstances that rob the believer of his peace when he forgets to believe and trust Jesus. I can assure you, my friends, that if I had to carry the burden of the MIDNIGHT CALL MINISTRY and everything that comes upon me in one day on my shoulders, I would have to be put in a psychiatric clinic immediately. I would not be able to sleep at all with the thought of the burden of it! But, my dear friend, Jesus Christ is a wonderful reality. Whoever believes in Him will not be put to shame. He will carry you along with all your burdens!

God has revealed to and in us the power of eternal life through Jesus Christ, and this is the peace which we have with God. *"For it is evident that our Lord sprang out of Juda...after the POWER OF AN ENDLESS LIFE"* (Hebrews 7:14,16). We are continually being rushed and agitated. We speak of progress, but the truth is that we are striding away from the peace of God and no longer know what it is to rest in His presence. If you will accept the Lord, who *"is now made manifest by the appearing of our Saviour Jesus Christ, who hath abolished death, and hath brought life and IMMORTALITY to light through the gospel"* (II Timothy 1:10), then you will find peace with God. You need to take hold of peace with God by taking hold of eternal life!

The Only Way to True Peace

You may ask: How can I do that? How can I receive eternal life? The answer: Jesus Christ Himself has made peace through His blood on the cross. There is no other way. Yet we hear the Lord's own words of sorrow in Romans 3:17, *"The way of peace have they not known."* The way of peace is unknown to most people.

What is the way to true peace? The answer is given by the Lord Himself, *"I am the way, the truth, and the*

Calvary, the only place where peace was established. Here, outside of the walls of Jerusalem, the Son of God proclaimed, "It is finished."

life: no man cometh unto the Father, but by me" (John 14:6).

People seek all sorts of ways to find peace and happiness, for instance, autogenous training, group dynamics, self-hypnosis, yoga, drugs, etc. Even many believers have to acknowledge that deep down they are still inconsistent and changeable. This is what it is like when your life is not on the firm foundation. Peace comes through building on the firm foundation. Whatever works are done on a changing foundation will have no lasting value. Those who have no peace with God never complete anything in their lives. They may begin a hundred things with great enthusiasm but they rarely finish anything. They continually miss their ultimate goal, the living God. Most people, whether in or outside the Church, long for something outside of themselves in which their roots can come to rest, but they are usually satisfied by things that produce temporary feelings. But this is not what we want. We want to enter that rest that God gives to His people as described in Hebrews 4:9-11, *"There remaineth therefore a rest to the people of God. For he that is entered into his rest, he also hath ceased from his own works, as God did from his. Let us labor therefore to enter into that rest, lest any man fall after the same example of unbelief."*

How often people try to hide their restlessness in excessive work. Some do reach impressive positions. Some achieve great honor. Others accumulate great riches. But one thing is lacking: true peace of heart. God warns against success as a camouflage for security. In Matthew 16:26, *"For what is a man profited, if he shall gain the whole world, and lose his own soul?"*

There are many ideals of man which may be impressive and sound wonderful but there is only one way of peace, if I may repeat it again, that is the peace with God through Jesus Christ.

Warning: False Peace!

All other avenues which man seeks to achieve peace with God come under the judgment, *"For our God is a consuming fire"* (Hebrews 12:29). The renowned philosopher R.W. Triene stated:

The simplest way to attain the undefeatable position is to begin searching for the unending sources of power and using the same instantly as one desires. I must continue to shine like a spotlight being connected to an inexhaustible power source, to oppose any attack, any attempt, which could cause disharmony within myself...

This infinite source of power is available here and now. Our true self is one with the life of God. That means infinite life and infinite power stands behind us. We only need to open the inner door to permit this power to flood our life and soul. Living in the recognition of truth brings peace, rich, remaining peace, which fulfills all of the present and future and gives us the assurance that we will remain strong as long as we live.

A way to peace without the Prince of Peace will end tragically, however. Especially in our day, man attempts to find another way of reaching inner harmony within himself; that is, he wants to be at rest with himself. He wants to reach the unreachable. He desires a never-ending source of strength, but all of these philosophies and attempts fail and will not lead to peace, but to utter desperation and eternal lostness. There are others who have recognized the inexhaustible source of joy and life in the living God but simply come to the conclusion that it is unreachable for them. They simply resign and state, "It is impossible for me to come to God." Others think that because God and man are so far apart, purely character-wise, there is no point in trying to reach Him. They resign themselves to what they consider to be unreachable.

Such people are weak-willed and everything is unreachable so they remain on this low level even as believers. Too often, such people are open to a false peace which is presented on a logical level. One such false way is propagated through the "Stoiker Epiket":

Let us realize our position. There are things which are within our powers. Other things are without our power. One thing stands within our power: namely, the decision to want or not to want. Nothing can hinder us to think or desire deep down in our heart the things we want. Not in our power is our body, our health, property, honor and career. Thus we must draw a line between these two areas and observe only those things which are within our power. Everything else is foreign. From that position, nothing can disturb our peace. If your only child dies, or the doctor confirms you have cancer, your business is on the verge of bankruptcy, you are about to lose your important job, whatever comes your way over which you have no control, simply state, 'All of it does not touch me. Nothing is being taken from me. I am just giving things back.'

Every discomfort, every disturbing incident of our mental balance originates with the power we have not. Therefore, act as if it is within our power.

When It Comes to Dying

Heinrich Heine, who was known for his anti-God mockery, did find peace at the end of his life through the Lord Jesus Christ. In one of his last poems, he wrote at the end:

When one lies on the deathbed, he becomes very sensitive and would like to make peace with God and the world. Because I myself am at the mercy of God, I have forgiven all of my adversaries. All my writings and poems that only had the slightest indication of any opposition against God, I have taken fearfully and burned them in the fire. It is better for these papers to burn than for him who wrote them.

Yes, I have made peace with my Creator, to the greatest offense of my 'enlightened' friends who accused me of backsliding into superstition, as they prefer to call my returning home to God. But I have returned to God like the prodigal son. For too long, I have fed the swine of the 'enlightened society.' Now, homesickness for heaven has overcome me. On the theological level, I have to confess to becoming a backslider: I have slidden back to a personal God!

It is important to point out here that not everyone will have the chance to find this grace on his deathbed, to find Jesus the Truth in his last moments. For that reason, the Word of God admonishes us; it even warns us so very seriously, *"Seek ye the Lord while He may be found, call ye upon Him while He is near"* (Isaiah 55:6).

This Is The Way. Walk Therein!

God judges very harshly every human psychological or religious way seeking peace outside the way of His Son, Jesus Christ. Man does not know the way of peace by himself, and God says through the prophet Isaiah in chapter 53:6, *"All we like sheep have gone astray; we have turned every one to his own way."* He condemns our own ways, but how thankful we are that this is not the final word, for that verse continues, *"and the Lord hath laid on him* [Jesus] *the iniquity of us all."* Jesus is the sin-bearer of the world, and He is the only way God has accepted. It is God's own way for you. If you are uneasy about yourself, if you recognize your own sinful nature, then surrender it to Jesus who carries the sins of the world. Then indeed you will experience

"the peace of God, which passeth all understanding"
(Philippians 4:7). There is no other way. All other
ways are our own ways. They are condemnable. They
lead to destruction, to eternal darkness. Choose today
this only way to true peace of heart.

Dear reader, be honest with yourself. Ask yourself
the question: What or who rules me? Is it fear,
jealousy, hate, wrath, evil thoughts? Do you have to
admit that evil desires rule your heart, and daily the
worries and the guilt which face you threaten to
destroy you? You know, it is really true. You are a poor
sinner! There is no need to hide behind your Christian
church, your traditional Christianity, for the devil
himself does not mind at all if you remain a church
member in good standing but without a personal
relationship with the Lord Jesus. One thing the enemy
does not want: namely, the fulfillment of the
Scripture such as Colossians 3:15, *"Let the peace of God
rule in your hearts,"* because whenever the peace of
God rules in your heart and life, then you have been
liberated from all resignation, from all the complica-
tion of your own created philosophies, and you are free
to serve a living and soon-returning God. Then the
dynamic power of God becomes effective in your life.
It is the peace of God with its unlimited power that
will enable you to live a life purposefully for God,
because your entire life will then be aimed at God.

Today, do not postpone your decision for Jesus
Christ. Remember, it may indeed be too late tomorrow.

Make use of it today, because if you really want the peace of God in your heart, then your must prepare now. There must be a change of authority in your heart and that change will determine eternity. To put it briefly, you either will spend eternity in everlasting, never-ending punishment or in never-ending eternal glory with your Lord. Therefore today, come to Him and in simple words tell Him, " Lord Jesus, come into my heart. Take over the rulership of my life. I am today surrendering it to you. Beginning now, you shall be my Prince of Peace."

News From Israel

This 32-page monthly magazine features articles written by the author of this book, Dr. Wim Malgo. It Biblically attempts to explain the relationship between Israel, the church, and their position in today's world. Many news features illuminated by God's Word in each issue makes this the magazine our subscribers READ from cover to cover. For your one-year subscription, send $7.00 to:

News From Israel
P.O. Box 4389
West Columbia, South Carolina 29171

FOR YOUR CONVENIENCE, THERE IS AN ORDER COUPON ON THE LAST PAGE OF THIS BOOK.

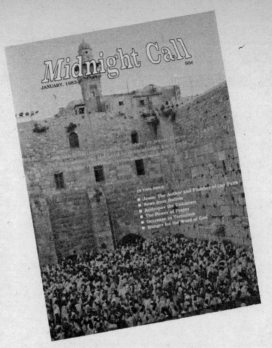

ORDER FORM

MAIL THIS ENTIRE PAGE TO:
MIDNIGHT CALL
P.O. BOX 4389, W. COLUMBIA, SC 29171

☐ Please send additional copies of this book, *In The Beginning Was The End:* ☐ 1 book: $4.95
☐ 5 books: $10.00 ☐ 10 books: $15.00
☐ 20 books: $20.00 ☐ 30 books: $25.00
☐ 40 books: $30.00 $_____

☐ Please begin a subscription to *Midnight Call* magazine for one year $_____

☐ Please begin a subscription to *News From Israel* magazine for one year $_____

Total Enclosed: $_____

Name _____

Address _____

City _____

State _____ Zip _____